# Writing Performance Counts

## Evaluate Your Writing

### . . . and Prepare for Writing Assessments

**Acknowledgments**
**Product Development:** Kent Publishing Services, Inc.
**Design and Production:** Signature Design Group, Inc.
**Photos:** 4, Joseph Sohm, ChromoSohm, Inc./Corbis; 5, Bill Losh/FPG International; 12, Jim Baron, Image Finders; 22, Corbis; 25, 26, 29, HWR Productions; 40, Wyane Lawler, Ecoscene/Corbis; 42, Todd Gipstein/Corbis; 46, Joseph Sohm, ChromoSohm, Inc./Corbis; 54, Yann Arthus-Bertrand/Corbis; 76, Araldo de Luca/Corbis; 77, Bettmann/Corbis; 81, Wally McNamee/Corbis; 98, Bettmann/Corbis; 100 Dave Bartruff/ Corbis

ISBN: 1-56936-794-9
Options Publishing, Inc.
P.O. Box 1749
Merrimack, NH 03054-1749
TOLL FREE: 800-782-7300 • FAX: 603-424-4056
www.optionspublishing.com

Printed in U.S.A.
15 14 13 12 11 10 9 8 7 6 5 4 3 2

# Table of Contents

**Lesson 1**

### Think and Read

➤ **Have you ever felt like you didn't fit into the crowd? Have you ever wanted to do something, but were too afraid to try because you might not be good enough? On the lines below, write down something that you'd like to do if you were guaranteed you'd be successful at it. Then read the narrative that follows.**

_____

_____

# TRYOUT

Shanika stood frozen by the water fountain. She stared at the swirling mass of red and white in the stands across the gym. The smell of dust and sweat stuffed her head. The student body was there to help judge the final auditions for the varsity cheerleading squad. An applause meter would choose new members. The pounding in her ears of the pep band drums was overpowered by a loud piercing screech of a microphone crackling.

"Number 35: Tenesha Woods, returning senior."

Shanika's stomach hit the floor when the students jumped to their feet. Tenesha bounded out to the center ring of the basketball court with two back handsprings and a back tuck. The crowd worshiped her as if she were a rock star as she stomped her feet and belted out the school fight cheer. When she was finished, she stepped up to the microphone and flashed the audience a playful grin.

"Hi! I'm Tenesha! I want to be a varsity cheerleader because I'm proud to be a Charger!"

Shanika's fingers trembled as she looked down at the three smudgy note cards she'd spent two hours writing the night before. Her sister had told her she was wasting her time. No one would ever want a new girl to be a cheerleader.

The beat of the stomping feet drove like spikes through the base of Shanika's neck. Shanika looked around at the rest of the girls still waiting to audition. They were busy tightening their ponytails and stretching their hamstrings for the mandatory splits. She marveled at how calm they all looked. She reached for her own ponytail, straightening the crisp red ribbon her sister had loaned her, insisting that Shanika didn't have a chance without it.

The idea of being a cheerleader had always intrigued Shanika, but she had never had the courage to even attend a pre-tryout practice at her old school. Actually, she had never auditioned for anything. She twisted the hem of her gym shorts into a tight fist, feeling her palm sweat through the nylon fabric. Looking around, she saw that she might look like one of these girls on the outside, but she couldn't believe they had tossed in bed for an hour before finally falling asleep as she had.

"Number 42: Shanika Adams, junior."

Shanika stood motionless as the silence in the gym hummed in her ears. She felt a nudge in her side, as a mouth full of braces smiled up at her and said, "Hey, that's your number."

Suddenly, Shanika felt her feet moving beneath her, barely touching the rubbery surface of the gym as she flipped repeatedly toward the center of the gym. She landed perfectly with a solid stick, and the crowd roared. The chanting and howling swirled around her.

Shanika walked to the microphone. Suddenly, her mind went blank. Why did she want to be a cheerleader? What should she say? She couldn't think of anything she'd written on her note cards. Pulsating blood rushed to her cheeks. Why, why, why?

## Prewriting and Referencing

▶ Corey's class was studying peer relationships. The students were asked to write a narrative about what happens when someone does not fit in with the crowd. Corey decided to write about what it would be like to not fit in.

To help him decide what he needed to know, Corey made a chart to demonstrate the problems that cause someone to have trouble fitting in. Look over his prewriting plans and answer questions 1–3.

| Not Fitting In | Fitting In |
| --- | --- |
| • Loneliness<br>• Being new/Not knowing anyone<br>• Not knowing the rules<br>• Not knowing the social customs<br>• Getting along easily with new people | • Outgoing personality<br>• Being considerate<br>• Being helpful |

1. Which of these ideas would BEST be added to the category "Not Fitting In"?

   Ⓐ Being kind to others          Ⓒ Being selfish

   Ⓑ Caring about others           Ⓓ Having a good sense of humor

2. Which one of these ideas does NOT belong in the category "Not Fitting In"?

   Ⓐ Not knowing the rules          Ⓒ Loneliness

   Ⓑ Being new/Not knowing anyone   Ⓓ Getting along easily with new people

3. Corey's chart did not have all the information he needed. Write three other ways to fit in with peers that Corey might discover in further research on the topic.

   _____

   _____

   _____

➤ **Use the following home page for the Web site _Teen Talk_ to answer questions 4–6.**

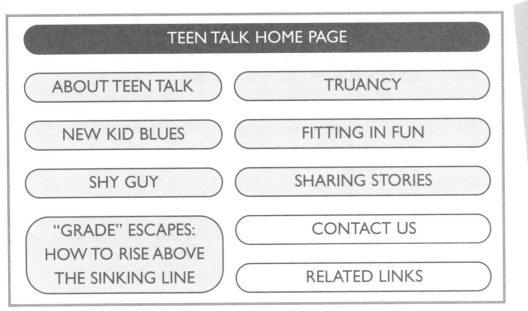

TEEN TALK HOME PAGE

ABOUT TEEN TALK

TRUANCY

NEW KID BLUES

FITTING IN FUN

SHY GUY

SHARING STORIES

"GRADE" ESCAPES: HOW TO RISE ABOVE THE SINKING LINE

CONTACT US

RELATED LINKS

### Writer's Tip

The prewriting and referencing stage is the time when you gather and organize information. Find out what you know about a topic. Then plan to research what you still must find out.

4. **Where could Corey BEST find information about the kinds of problems new kids face?**

Ⓐ Shy Guy

Ⓒ About Teen Talk

Ⓑ Fitting in Fun

Ⓓ New Kid Blues

5. **How could Corey BEST find information to better understand kids who are truant from school?**

Ⓐ New Kid Blues

Ⓒ Truancy

Ⓑ "Grade" Escapes: How to Rise Above the Sinking Line

Ⓓ Contact Us

6. **Where could Corey get personal accounts of real teen challenges?**

Ⓐ Sharing Stories

Ⓒ Related Links

Ⓑ Contact Us

Ⓓ Fitting in Fun

In a comparison chart, a writer lists two or more categories. A writer brainstorms for ideas to complete comparison charts. Which questions ask about extra information needed to complete the chart? Talk it over with a friend.

Lesson 2: Prewriting and Referencing

➤ **Now check your answers. If you answered a question incorrectly, study the correct answer.**

1. **Which of these ideas would BEST be added to the category "Not Fitting In"?**

   Answer Ⓒ is the correct answer. Selfishness is not an admirable trait. Kindness, caring, and humor are traits that would help someone fit in with others.

2. **Which one of these ideas does NOT belong in the category "Not Fitting In"?**

   Answer Ⓓ is the correct answer. Getting along easily with new people is not an obstacle to fitting in with others.

3. **Corey's chart did not have all the information he needed. Write three other ways to fit in with peers that Corey might discover in further research on the topic.**

   **Examples may include:**
   receptive attitude toward others' ideas, shared interests with others, willingness to help others

4. **Where could Corey BEST find information about the kinds of problems new kids face?**

   Answer Ⓓ is correct. *Blues* refers to feeling low or sad. This page will most likely provide information about specific problems new kids face.

5. **How could Corey BEST find information to better understand kids who are truant from school?**

   Answer Ⓒ is correct. *Truancy* addresses the issues involved with kids who regularly skip school.

6. **Where could Corey get personal accounts of real teen challenges?**

   Answer Ⓐ is correct. *Sharing Stories* would allow individuals to ask questions and respond personally.

# Try It

➤ Here is a chance to work on your prewriting and referencing skills. Answer the questions on the next three pages.

1. Look at the Teen Talk Home Page choices again on page 7. List the option that you probably wouldn't use to research "Fitting In."

_____

2. How could Corey find professional opinions and advice about teens having trouble fitting in?

_____

_____

_____

3. How could Corey begin a new Web search on the topic of "Not Fitting In"? Which keyword or words could he use to begin the search?

_____

_____

4. Consider the possibility that fitting in is not always the best goal. What are some ways that kids try to fit in, but hurt themselves or others by doing so? List two ways below.

_____

_____

_____

Lesson 2: Prewriting and Referencing

**5.** Where could Corey look to find information about when it is a good idea to try to fit in with the crowd? List as many sources as you can.

_____

_____

_____

_____

**6.** Sometimes students act in certain ways to try to fit in. For each effect below, list what you think the cause might be. For example, Erin plays the class clown in Spanish class to conceal that she's actually getting all As.

| Cause | | Effect |
|-------|---|--------|
| | → | student is late for class |
| | → | student joins the drama club |
| | → | student makes a list of the school subjects he likes |
| | → | student makes an appointment with her guidance counselor at school |

**7.** Who could Corey ask for advice to help him write his narrative?

Ⓐ another student

Ⓑ his principal

Ⓒ his parents

Ⓓ any of the above

8. How could Corey find information about the consequences of loneliness using the card catalog at the school library?

_____

_____

_____

9. Bringing your own experience to narratives can make them more real to your readers. Think about the times you did fit in, and the times you didn't. Complete the chart like Corey's below.

| Times I Fit In | Times I Didn't Fit In |
| --- | --- |
|  |  |

10. What else would your readers like to know about your experience of fitting in? List two items below.

_____

_____

_____

_____

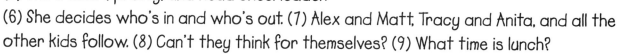

▶ **Read this part of Corey's rough draft of his narrative. Then answer questions 1–7.**

(1) Dear Diary...

(2) Today was a rough day?
(3) I knew it was going to be tough fitting in to Piedmont Junior high, but I never would have guessed. (4) Krystal is the most popular girl in school. (5) She's smart, pretty, and head cheerleader. (6) She decides who's in and who's out. (7) Alex and Matt, Tracy and Anita, and all the other kids follow. (8) Can't they think for themselves? (9) What time is lunch?

(10) Today, the lunchtime bell rang and I knew I would eat by myself in the corner of the cafeteria. (11) I mean, I would sit here by myself. (12) I'll just watch the other kids laughing, gossiping, and having fun.

(13) So, there I was. (14) I will be staring at my food as I walk to my seat. (15) Then, right before I got to my seat in the corner, it happened. (16) I tripped on the leg of Krystal's chair as I walked by and my tray of food went flying to the floor. (17) Krystal spun around to see what had happened. (18) In stead of the usual scene, all I saw was a sea of laughing faces, all staring at me. (19) And right there in front of me, front row center, was Krystal. (20) "What's your problem?" she sneered and looked for approval in Tracy's eyes. (21) The laughing stopped, it was as if the whole cafeteria waited to see what would happen next.

1. **Sentence 2 has a punctuation error. Rewrite the sentence using the correct punctuation.**

_____

_____

2. **Which sentence does not belong in this passage?**

    Ⓐ sentence 3         Ⓒ sentence 19

    Ⓑ sentence 9         Ⓓ sentence 20

3. Sentence 7 is a fragment. Write a new ending that tells us about the object of the sentence.

_____

_____

4. Which sentence is not in Corey's first-person voice?

Ⓐ I thought it was going to be . . .

Ⓑ So, there I was.

Ⓒ Krystal spun around to see . . .

Ⓓ Instead of the usual scene, all I saw . . .

5. Which sentence is redundant, or repeats information?

Ⓐ sentence 11

Ⓑ sentence 14

Ⓒ sentence 18

Ⓓ sentence 20

6. Corey shifts verb tenses between sentences 13 and 14. The tense shifts from—

Ⓐ past to future.

Ⓑ present to past.

Ⓒ past to past progressive.

Ⓓ past progressive to past.

7. Sentence 21 contains two ideas. Revise the sentence so it is two complete sentences.

_____

_____

**Writer's Tip**

Too many short sentences can make your writing sound too simple. To add variety and complexity to your writing, try to avoid using too many simple sentences.

**Noodle Around**

In first drafts, a writer can change the verb tenses—the time the action happens. But too many changes in tense can confuse readers. Which question asks about verb tenses? Discuss your answer with a friend.

Lesson 3: Composing and Revising

➤ **Now check your answers. If you answered a question incorrectly, study the correct answer.**

1. **Sentence 2 has a punctuation error. Rewrite the sentence using the correct punctuation.**

   The sentence makes a statement. It should end with a period or exclamation point.
   Today was a rough day.

2. **Which sentence does not belong in this passage?**

   Answer Ⓑ is correct. Lunchtime is not relevant to the story.

3. **Sentence 7 is a fragment. Write a new ending that tells us about the object of the sentence.**

   Your rewrite should not change the outcome of the story. For example:
   Alex and Matt, Tracy and Anita, and all the other kids follow Krystal's rules.

4. **Which sentence is not in Corey's first-person voice?**

   Answer Ⓓ is the correct answer. This sentence switches to third person.

5. **Which sentence is redundant, or not necessary?**

   Answer Ⓐ is the correct answer. We know that the writer will sit alone.

6. **Corey shifts verb tenses between sentences 13 and 14. The tense shifts from—**

   The correct answer is Ⓐ. Corey shifts from past to future tense by using the words *will be staring*.

7. **Sentence 21 contains two ideas. Revise the sentence so it is two complete sentences.**

   Two independent clauses must be separated by a period. The sentence should be revised as follows:
   The laughing stopped. It was as if the whole cafeteria waited to see what would happen next.

# Try It

> **Here is a chance to work on your composing and revising skills. Answer the questions on the next three pages.**

1. **Here are some more examples of different voices. Label each as first-, second-, or third-person voice.**

   **a.** You wouldn't believe how loud the music was. _____

   **b.** Shane covered his ears when the microphone screeched. _____

   **c.** I have never heard anything so loud in my life! _____

   **d.** Linda tried to explain why she was late. _____

2. **Read the following pairs of sentences. Write *redundant* after any pair that repeats itself.**

   **a.** You are so smart. You are really intelligent. _____

   **b.** I want pizza for dinner. For dessert I want ice cream. _____

   **c.** Baseball is not my favorite sport. Basketball is the greatest. _____

   **d.** Speak to me! Talk to me! _____

3. **Combine the following sentences to improve the level of writing. Be sure to use proper punctuation.**

   **a.** She was the fastest swimmer. She set a new record.

   _____

   **b.** We hardly ever eat pasta. I really like pasta.

   _____

   **c.** Go get the ball. The ball is in the mud.

   _____

   **d.** Tomorrow is New Year's Eve. I love New Year's Eve.

   _____

Lesson 3: Composing and Revising

**4. Sentence fragments leave the reader hanging. Combine the following fragments to make one complete sentence.**

**a.** She needs some money. To go to the movies.

_____

**b.** And I don't like to watch my brother swim. But my mom made me go.

_____

**c.** Jump over. If the fence isn't that high.

_____

**5. Use your revising skills to check all punctuation. Add proper punctuation to the following run-on sentences using these editing symbols:** $\wedge$ **and** $\odot$

**a.** I have homework to do and I can't go to the game until I finish it

**b.** I wish I had a car to drive to the game so I could make it in time before the kickoff

**c.** Have you ever gotten up late and you missed the bus and then you got a tardy slip for first period

**d.** Last year I studied math science social studies and English

**6. Writing that changes verb tenses can confuse the reader. Read each pair of sentences below. Write _shift_ after each pair that shifts tenses.**

**a.** I ate in a hurry. I feel sick. _____

**b.** I ate in a hurry. I felt sick. _____

**c.** She is eating in a hurry. She was feeling sick. _____

**d.** Are you hungry? Did you eat that? _____

7. **Writing in the present tense gives your reader a sense that the action is happening right now. Rewrite the following sentences to be in the present tense.**

   **a.** The water was so cold!

   _____

   **b.** The kids jumped into the water.

   _____

   **c.** Matt tried to climb the rope, but he fell.

   _____

8. **Poor writing can distract the reader. Rewrite the following poorly written sentences to correct errors of punctuation and tense.**

   **a.** She wanted to go to the park but I'm not going.

   _____

   **b.** We ate pizza, roller-blading and walked around town.

   _____

   **c.** My job is getting the newspapers, throw them on the lawns, to do it before 7:00.

   _____

   **d.** Tomorrow, I'll go ice-skating tonight.

   _____

9. **Future tense suggests what will happen in the future. Write *future* on the line next to any sentence below that is written in the future tense.**

   **a.** Michael was early for practice. _____

   **b.** Michael will be late for practice. _____

   **c.** Michael was not early for practice. _____

Read the rest of Corey's rough draft of his narrative. Notice the groups of underlined words. Questions 1–7 will ask about them.

(22) I <u>try</u> to become invisible by kneeling down to pick up what was left of my lunch sprawled on the floor. (23) As I reached for the slimy, ketchup-coated hotdog, <u>they</u> noticed another hand grabbing for it. (24) <u>I shouldn't have not let it happen,</u> but my heart began to race even faster in fear. (25) What humiliating thing would happen to me next? (26) As I looked up, I was amazed at what I saw. (27) It was Tracy helping me pick up the mess.

(28) The look in Krystal's eye's said enough. (29) But of course, it wasn't enough. (30) "Hey Tracy, she said, "I <u>don't</u> know you hung out with clumsy nerds. (31) The cafeteria was dead quiet now, and the comment caught Tracy a little off-guard. (32) The tension was building, and nobody knew what was going to <u>happen next I guess</u> that's why Mrs. Martinez, our Assistant Principal, was quickly making her way toward the scene.

(33) "I hear the school is taking applications for a new janitor. Maybe you should take the job, Tracy," Krystal blurted out with a sarcastic giggle. (34) It was showdown time. (35) A circle of kids surrounded us, all eager for a ringside view.

(36) I could tell Tracy was confused and not sure what to do next (37) Beads of sweat were trickling down my beet-red face. (38) Finally, Tracy said, "Cool idea. Then I could take all my friends out to the movies this weekend. Who wants to go?" (39) There was a huge roar and everybody's hand shot up, except for Krystal's of course. (40) It was amazing. (41) At that moment, Tracy become the leader of school. (42) Mrs. Martinez slowly backed away from the crowd. (43) She knew she would have to have a talk with Krystal later in the day.

**1.** How should Corey edit the underlined part of sentence 22?

   Ⓐ trying          Ⓒ have

   Ⓑ tried           Ⓓ no changes needed

2. **How should Corey edit the underlined part of sentence 23 to correct the pronoun problem?**

   Ⓐ she

   Ⓑ we

   Ⓒ I

   Ⓓ me

3. **Sentence 24 has a double negative. How should Corey edit it?**

   _____

   _____

4. **How should Corey edit the underlined part of sentence 30?**

   Ⓐ haven't

   Ⓑ didn't

   Ⓒ wouldn't

   Ⓓ no changes needed

5. **How should Corey correct the punctuation in sentence 30?**

   _____

   _____

6. **How should Corey edit the underlined part of sentence 32?**

   Ⓐ happen next, I guess…

   Ⓑ happen next. I guess…

   Ⓒ happen next: I guess…

   Ⓓ no change needed

7. **How should Corey edit sentence 41?**

   _____

   _____

Lesson 4: Editing

# Analyze Your Answers | Editing

➤ **Now check your answers. If you answered a question incorrectly, study the correct answer.**

1. **How should Corey edit the underlined part of sentence 22?**

   Answer Ⓑ is the correct answer. The story is written in the past tense. *Tried* is the past tense of *try*.

2. **How should Corey edit the underlined part of sentence 23 to correct the pronoun problem?**

   Answer Ⓒ is the correct answer. The pronoun *I* is correct.

3. **Sentence 24 has a double negative. How should Corey edit it?**

   Corey should rewrite the sentence as follows:

   I should not have let it happen, but my heart began to race even faster in fear.

4. **How should Corey edit the underlined part of sentence 30?**

   Answer Ⓑ is correct. Cory should replace *don't* with *didn't*.

5. **How should Corey correct the punctuation in sentence 30?**

   Corey should correct the punctuation as follows.

   "Hey Tracy," she said. "I didn't know you hung out with clumsy nerds."

6. **How should Corey edit the underlined part of sentence 32?**

   Answer Ⓑ is correct. The sentence is a run on. The first sentence needs a period after *next*.

7. **How should Corey edit sentence 41?**

   Cory should change the word *become* to *became* to stay in the past tense.

   At that moment, Tracy became the leader of the school.

# Try It

> **Here is a chance to work on your editing skills. Answer the questions on the next three pages.**

1. Review these sentences which use words that might "sound" right, but they are not. Rewrite the sentences using the correct words.

   **a.** I'm not goin to the movie. _____

   **b.** We should of had pizza for dinner. _____

   **c.** I was kinda scared when the lights went out. _____

   **d.** It was sorta like the circus, but with no animals. _____

2. **Here is another example of pronoun confusion. Edit and rewrite the sentence so that it is clear.**

   Lonna and Brittney were walking down the hall when she dropped her books.

   _____

   _____

3. Here are some more run-on sentences. Rewrite them using proper punctuation.

   **a.** I have trained hard for this event and I am ready to compete.

   _____

   **b.** The flowers in the vase are roses, the blooms are pink and yellow.

   _____

   **c.** The mountain has the highest peak in the world its peak has taken many climbers' lives.

   _____

   **d.** I'm going to bake cookies and then I'm going to eat the whole batch!

   _____

4. **Punctuation errors detract from good writing. The following sentence has a punctuation error. Rewrite it to make it correct.**

Mr and Mrs. Johnson ate dinner at Jim's house tonight.

_____

5. **The following sentence is missing an apostrophe. Add the apostrophe to correct it. Use this editing symbol ∨.**

The Cougars are the best team in the citys baseball league.

6. **Here is an example of a sentence that uses a double negative. Rewrite it to make it correct.**

We aren't going nowhere without our bikes.

_____

7. **Usage errors confuse readers. Which sentence below has a usage error? Rewrite the sentence to correct the error.**

Ⓐ Do you want to go to the library today?

Ⓑ When are you gonna go home after school?

Ⓒ She and I are planning a party.

_____

8. **Here are some sentences that have contraction errors. Rewrite each sentence to make it correct.**

   **a.** She ca'nt come with us today.

   _____

   **b.** You shouldnt' eat too many sweets before dinner.

   _____

   **c.** Havent you ever received a package in the mail?

   _____

9. **Look for errors of usage and punctuation. Rewrite the following sentence to make it correct.**

   My best friend isn't never going to take karate lessons with me cause shes afraid.

   _____

   _____

10. **Informal writing uses slang, which can lower your score for word choice and creativity. Replace each informal word with its formal equivalent.**

    **a.** nope _____

    **b.** youse _____

    **c.** could of _____

    **d.** yeah _____

➤ **Now you are going to read and evaluate another narrative that Corey wrote. It is about a student who tries to fit in with his family. Before you begin, read the checklist below.**

# Writing Checklist

Corey will earn his best score if he achieves the following goals:

| | |
|---|---|
| **Ideas** | • Ideas are original<br>• Topic is clearly identified<br>• Ideas support the topic |
| **Organization** | • Ideas are related and presented in correct order<br>• Strong beginning, middle, and end |
| **Creativity and Word Choice** | • Words used appropriately<br>• Creative descriptions<br>• Words enhance ideas |
| **Sentence Structure** | • Complete sentences<br>• Clearly written and easy to understand |
| **Spelling and Punctuation** | • Few or no errors |

➤ **Read the directions Corey was given.**

**Directions:** Every person has a position in a family, whether it is being the oldest, youngest, middle, foster, or adopted child. Feeling like you fit into a family can sometimes be a challenge, especially for the middle child. Write a letter from a parent to a middle child that would help the child feel like his or her position is a special one.

# The Magical Middle

(1) It won't be long now until you will be venturing off to high school. (2) You used to make the biggest racket with the pots and pans when you played parade. (3) It seems like just yesterday that you were a baby, crawling around the kitchen. (4) You were always the one who liked to lead the others, even though you weren't the oldest child. (5) Everyone used to joke that you would grow up to be a movie director, telling everyone else what to do. (6) The wonderful thing about you is that others have always followed you willingly. (7) You the type of leaders that people wants to follow and it seems to come so natural for you. (8) That is a special gift that many people try to cultivate.

(9) I know that it's not always easy to be the middle child. (10) Tricia has always been the first to do everything. (11) She was the first to go off to school, leaving you home with only Becca for a playmate. (12) She started swimming lessons and girl scouts, and all you ever heard was, "Wait until you're older."

## Writer's Tip

Every detail in a short narrative is important. Details quickly establish the mood and feeling of the piece. As you read this personal narrative, pay close attention to the details, and ask yourself why the author chose to include them.

(13) Now she can drive, going out on dates, and had got a part-time job. (14) It must seem like she has all the privileges, and you have none. (15) You will enjoy those same privileges when you are her age. (16) Just remember that she was your age once, too. (17) There was a time when you can't wait to be the age you are right now.

(18) So, maybe you're thinking that being the oldest wouldn't be so great after all. But, does being the youngest seem even better? (19) No, Danny. (20) I think you've got the best position in the family line-up. (21) Sure, Becca get a lots of attention cause she the youngest. (22) You might even think that we spoil her. (23) If, you could only see the way how much she admires you though. (24) You have always been there for her. (25) From the day she was born, you have been her friend. (26) She knows that one day, not so far away, you will be heading off into the world, leaving her home alone. (27) You will go off to new adventures, and she will miss you terribly. (28) You have never been without a sibling, without a friend. (29) You, Danny, are the lucky one.

(30) There are actually many advantages to being the middle child. (31) Tricia is our test case child, and she has to put up with all the mistakes that new parents make. (32) By the time you come along, your mom and I are old pros. (33) You are always so laid back and relaxed. (34) That's probably because your parents aren't totally stressed out the second time around at parenting!

(35) A sibling is a brother or a sister. (36) The best advice for him as he starts his journey through his high school years is to live each day to its fullest. (37) He shouldn't be in such a hurry to grow up!

Love, Dad

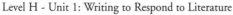

➤ **Now answer the questions about Corey's narrative.**

1. Corey's narrative is written in the style of a letter, otherwise known as "epistolary" writing. The narrative needs a proper greeting for an introduction. Write a greeting for Corey to include on the line below.

   _____

2. Sentence 2 is not in the correct sequence. Which one of the sentences would it BEST follow?

   Ⓐ sentence 3          Ⓒ sentence 6

   Ⓑ sentence 5          Ⓓ sentence 7

3. Sentence 13 has usage errors. The verbs should be written in the same tense. Rewrite the sentence correctly on the lines below.

   _____

   _____

4. Sentence 17 has a shift in verb tense. How should it be edited to make it correct?

   _____

   _____

5. The paragraph that begins with sentence 18 is out of sequence. Which paragraph should it follow?

   Ⓐ the paragraph that begins with sentence 1

   Ⓑ the paragraph that begins with sentence 9

   Ⓒ the paragraph that begins with sentence 30

   Ⓓ the paragraph that begins with sentence 35

# Evaluate Corey's Writing

6. **Sentence 19 is an incomplete sentence, or fragment. Combine the sentence with sentence 20 so it is complete.**

_____

_____

7. **Sentence 21 is poorly written. Which one of these choices is the BEST way to rewrite it?**

Ⓐ Sure Becca gets lots of attention because she the youngest.

Ⓑ Sure, Becca get a lot of attention cause she is the youngest.

Ⓒ Sure, Becca do get a lot of attention cause she been the youngest.

Ⓓ Sure, Becca gets a lot of attention because she is the youngest.

8. **Sentence 23 is poorly written. Rewrite the sentence so it has proper usage and punctuation.**

_____

_____

9. **The paragraph that begins with sentence 30 shifts into present tense. Edit the sentences in the paragraph to better fit with the rest of the narrative.**

_____

_____

_____

_____

_____

_____

**10.** Which sentence does not belong in this narrative?

    Ⓐ sentence 35

    Ⓑ sentence 30

    Ⓒ sentence 9

    Ⓓ sentence 1

**11.** Sentence 7 is not written properly. Write it correctly on the lines below.

_____

_____

**12.** The last paragraph shifts out of the second-person voice and into third-person voice. Edit the sentences in the paragraph to better fit with the rest of the narrative.

_____

_____

_____

_____

_____

_____

              Lesson 5: Evaluate Writing

# Evaluate Corey's Writing

➤ **Here is a guide for evaluating writing called a rubric. Rubrics are used to grade writing tests. Use this rubric to rate Corey's narrative.**

# Writing Rubric

| Score | Ideas | Organization | Creativity and Word Choice | Sentence Structure | Spelling and Punctuation |
|---|---|---|---|---|---|
| **4** | • Ideas are original<br>• Topic is clearly identified<br>• Ideas support the topic | • Ideas are related and presented in correct order<br>• Strong beginning, middle, and end | • Words used appropriately<br>• Creative descriptions<br>• Words enhance ideas | • Complete sentences<br>• Clearly written and easy to understand | • Few or no errors |
| **3** | • Some ideas are original<br>• Most ideas support the topic | • Most ideas are related and presented in correct order<br>• Good beginning, middle, and end | • Most words used appropriately<br>• Some creative descriptions<br>• Words support ideas | • Many sentences are complete<br>• Most sentences are clearly written and easy to understand | • Some errors |
| **2** | • Few ideas are original<br>• Ideas wander from topic<br>• Some details support the topic | • Some ideas are related and presented in correct order<br>• Weak beginning, middle, and end | • Some words used appropriately<br>• Few creative descriptions | • Some run-on or fragmented sentences<br>• Some sentences are unclear | • Many errors |
| **1** | • Ideas are incomplete<br>• Few details support the topic | • Few ideas are related and presented in correct order<br>• No real beginning, middle, and end | • Few words used appropriately<br>• No attempt at creative descriptions | • Several run-on or fragmented sentences<br>• Many sentences are unclear | • Serious errors |
| **0** | • No attempt | • No attempt | • No attempt | • No attempt | • No attempt |

➤ **Give Corey's writing a score of 0 to 4 for each category. Explain why you gave him that score.**

[ ]
score

Ideas _____

_____

_____

[ ]
score

Organization _____

_____

_____

[ ]
score

Creativity and Word Choice _____

_____

_____

[ ]
score

Sentence Structure _____

_____

_____

[ ]
score

Spelling and Punctuation _____

_____

Lesson 5: Evaluate Writing

➤ **Now it is your turn to write about a topic. Read the directions below. Then re**
**the checklist that you and your teacher will use to rate your writing.**

**Directions:** Consider how you fit into your peer group. Write a narrative that demonstrates th
challenges of fitting in with a crowd. Be sure your narrative is well organized and uses words th
make your writing clear.

## Writing Checklist

I will earn my best score if I achieve the following goals:

| | |
|---|---|
| **Ideas** | • Ideas are original<br>• Topic is clearly identified<br>• Ideas support the topic |
| **Organization** | • Ideas are related and presented in correct order<br>• Strong beginning, middle, and end |
| **Creativity and Word Choice** | • Words used appropriately<br>• Creative descriptions<br>• Words enhance ideas |
| **Sentence Structure** | • Complete sentences<br>• Clearly written and easy to understand |
| **Spelling and Punctuation** | • Few or no errors |

# Plan Your Writing

➤ **Use these pages to plan your writing. You may find this graphic organizer helpful.**

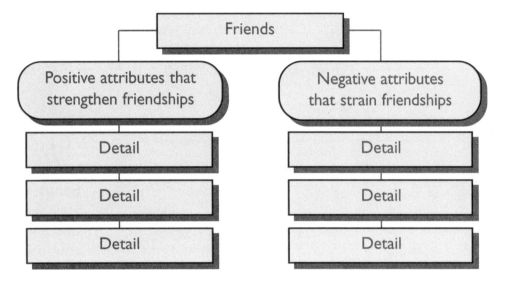

_____

_____

_____

_____

_____

_____

_____

_____

_____

_____

_____

_____

_____

# Writer's Tip

When planning your writing, try to think of the main points you want to make. Organize your writing so that you end with a strong point. Ending on a weak point will affect your reader's overall impression of the writing.

_____

_____

_____

_____

_____

_____

_____

_____

_____

## Writer's Tip

Before you proofread your work, make a list of common mistakes you make. Read your work, checking for one type of mistake at a time.

_____

_____

_____

_____

_____

_____

_____

_____

_____

_____

## Writer's Tip

Unless there is a specific reason to change verb tense, it is best to remain consistent throughout a piece of writing to avoid reader confusion.

# Write Your Final Draft

**➤ Use all the skills you have learned in this unit to score well on your final draft. Remember to carefully proofread your work before you give it to your teacher.**

1 _____

2 _____

3 _____

4 _____

5 _____

6 _____

7 _____

8 _____

9 _____

10 _____

11 _____

12 _____

13 _____

14 _____

15 _____

16 _____

17 _____

18 _____

19 _____

20 _____

21 _____

22 _____

23 _____

24 _____

25 _____

26 _____

27 _____

28 _____

29 _____

30 _____

31 _____

32 _____

33 _____

34 _____

35 _____

36 _____

37 _____

38 _____

39 _____

40 _____

41 _____

42 _____

43 _____

44 _____

45 _____

Lesson 6: Your Turn to Write

> **Here is the same rubric you used to evaluate Corey's narrative. Use it to evaluate your writing.**

# Writing Rubric

| Score | Ideas | Organization | Creativity and Word Choice | Sentence Structure | Spelling and Punctuation |
|---|---|---|---|---|---|
| **4** | • Ideas are original<br>• Topic is clearly identified<br>• Ideas support the topic | • Ideas are related and presented in correct order<br>• Strong beginning, middle, and end | • Words used appropriately<br>• Creative descriptions<br>• Words enhance ideas | • Complete sentences<br>• Clearly written and easy to understand | • Few or no errors |
| **3** | • Some ideas are original<br>• Most ideas support the topic | • Most ideas are related and presented in correct order<br>• Good beginning, middle, and end | • Most words used appropriately<br>• Some creative descriptions<br>• Words support ideas | • Many sentences are complete<br>• Most sentences are clearly written and easy to understand | • Some errors |
| **2** | • Few ideas are original<br>• Ideas wander from topic<br>• Some details support the topic | • Some ideas are related and presented in correct order<br>• Weak beginning, middle, and end | • Some words used appropriately<br>• Few creative descriptions | • Some run-on or fragmented sentences<br>• Some sentences are unclear | • Many errors |
| **1** | • Ideas are incomplete<br>• Few details support the topic | • Few ideas are related and presented in correct order<br>• No real beginning, middle, and end | • Few words used appropriately<br>• No attempt at creative descriptions | • Several run-on or fragmented sentences<br>• Many sentences are unclear | • Serious errors |
| **0** | • No attempt | • No attempt | • No attempt | • No attempt | • No attempt |

➤ **Give your own writing a score of 0 to 4 for each category. Explain why you gave yourself that score.**

[ ]
score

Ideas _____

_____

_____

_____

[ ]
score

Organization _____

_____

_____

_____

[ ]
score

Creativity and Word Choice _____

_____

_____

_____

[ ]
score

Sentence Structure _____

_____

_____

_____

[ ]
score

Spelling and Punctuation _____

_____

_____

Lesson 6: Your Turn to Write

**Lesson 1**

➤ **Living in our modern world of computers, television, and cell phones, you might think the great outdoors is not quite as important as it once was. Think for a moment what life would be like without trees. On the lines below, write down all the things you use in your life that come from trees. Then read the article that follows.**

---

---

# Nature in **Danger**

It doesn't take a tree to make a computer start up, and a tropical flower can't help send a cell phone call. So, do we really need plants anymore? The answer is clearly, Yes! Without plant life, human life would end. Without vegetation, people would lose natural resources, such as food, paper, lumber, and other important products from the Earth. Most importantly, people would not be able to breathe without plant life. Plants require the carbon dioxide that animals exhale, and animals inhale the oxygen that plants release. Without each other, plant and animal life would end!

Did you know that every minute, more than one hundred acres of rain forest are destroyed on Earth? Many factors cause the destruction, or "deforestation," of the Earth's natural resources. One factor is population. As the Earth's population grows, there is a greater need for more products from nature. More crops are needed to feed, clothe, and provide housing for people. This means that more of the Earth's natural forestland must be used for growing crops. This results in deforestation. While forests are shrinking to make room for new crops, the growing population needs more housing. That means less room to plant replacement trees.

Another factor that causes deforestation is politics. Many countries have laws that protect trees and limit the amount of land development. However, in some countries, many species of plant and animal life are in danger because land development is not controlled. Every day, up to one hundred species of plants and animals die out due to deforestation.

Finally, attitudes and values contribute to the deforestation of the Earth. Many people feel that the need for food, clothing, and housing is more important than the need to protect the Earth's natural resources. Many landowners are influenced by the opportunity to make large amounts of money from cash crops. It is difficult for some people to accept the reality of the terrible effects that deforestation can cause. It is easier and more enjoyable to live in the present moment than it is to protect forests.

## Ways You Can Help

There are many ways at school and at home you can help stop the spread of deforestation.

- Don't waste paper at school.
- Use both sides of a sheet of paper.
- Use scrap paper whenever you can.
- Choose 100 percent post-consumer recycled paper or "tree-free" paper.
- Use cloth napkins and real plates instead of paper napkins and paper plates.
- Use cloth towels instead of paper towels to wipe up spills.
- Recycle newspapers and old school papers.
- Don't print out e-mail.
- Send e-mail greetings rather than greeting cards for special occasions.
- Read books and newspapers online where possible.

Today, we might think we do not need plants anymore. But, just like the World Wide Web, our physical world is a large, connected web, too. Every time you choose to do one of the things listed above, you help curb deforestation and save our plants. And we all know that we need our plants to survive!

➤ **Christine's teacher asked each of her students to persuade readers that recycling is beneficial. Christine decided to write about paper recycling.**

**To help her decide what she needed to know, Christine started writing this outline about paper recycling. Read the outline and use it to answer questions 1–3.**

## Paper Recycling

I.   Where do trees used for paper production grow?

II.   What would happen if we didn't recycle?

III.

IV.   What types of paper are best for art classes?

V.

VI.   What can I do to recycle paper?

VII.   What is the difference between recyclable paper and recycled paper?

VIII.   How is paper recycled?

1. **Which of these ideas would BEST be added as section III.?**

   Ⓐ What alternatives are there to paper production from trees?

   Ⓑ Where can you get the best prices for paper?

   Ⓒ How do they make paper different colors?

   Ⓓ What is the best type of saw for chopping down trees?

2. **Which one of these ideas does NOT belong in Christine's outline?**

   Ⓐ I.                      Ⓒ IV.

   Ⓑ II.                     Ⓓ VI.

3. **Write two questions that Christine could ask someone who works at a recycling facility to find out more about deforestation and recycling.**

   _____

   _____

**Use the home page display of the Web site *Save the Earth* to answer questions 4–7.**

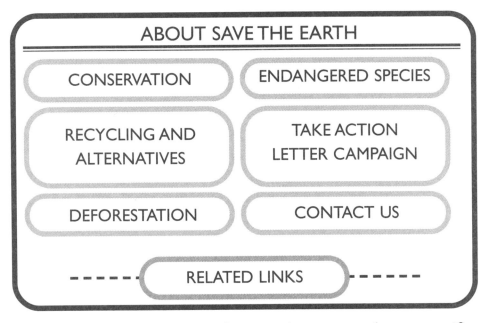

ABOUT SAVE THE EARTH

CONSERVATION

ENDANGERED SPECIES

RECYCLING AND ALTERNATIVES

TAKE ACTION LETTER CAMPAIGN

DEFORESTATION

CONTACT US

RELATED LINKS

4. **Where should Christine go online to ask someone about a specific question in her research?**

   Ⓐ Take Action Letter Campaign

   Ⓑ About Save the Earth

   Ⓒ Contact Us

   Ⓓ Related Links

5. **How could Christine BEST find more in-depth information about a topic covered only briefly at this site?**

   Ⓐ Take Action Letter Campaign

   Ⓑ Recycling and Alternatives

   Ⓒ Contact Us

   Ⓓ Related Links

6. **Which button should Christine select to find information about "tree-free" or recycled paper?**

   Ⓐ Deforestation

   Ⓑ Recycling and Alternatives

   Ⓒ Conservation

   Ⓓ Endangered Species

7. **Where would Christine LIKELY find information about contacting her political representatives?**

   Ⓐ Contact Us

   Ⓑ Related Links

   Ⓒ Take Action Letter Campaign

   Ⓓ About Save the Earth

**Writer's Tip**

If you are searching for information on a specific topic, check to see how many pages are given to the topic before choosing a book as a resource.

**Noodle Around**

Writers often use outlines to organize their ideas. But writers sometimes list unrelated topic ideas. Which question asks you about unrelated topic ideas? Talk it over with a friend.

Lesson 2: Prewriting and Referencing

➤ **Now check your answers. If you answered a question incorrectly, study the correct answer.**

1. **Which of these ideas would BEST be added to section III.?**

   Answer Ⓐ is the correct answer. Christine's outline relates to the problems associated with deforestation and the need to recycle.

2. **Which one of these ideas does NOT belong in Christine's outline?**

   Answer Ⓒ is the correct answer because IV. is not related to the topic of recycling.

3. **Write two questions that Christine could ask someone who works at a recycling facility to find out more about deforestation and recycling.**

   What are the steps involved in making recycled paper? What is the difference between 100 percent post-consumer recycling and other types of recycling?

4. **Where should Christine go online to ask someone about a specific question in her research?**

   The correct answer is Ⓒ. By selecting the *Contact Us* icon, Christine will find information about contacting the site directly.

5. **How could Christine BEST find more in-depth information about a topic covered only briefly at this site?**

   Answer Ⓓ is correct. *Related Links* will provide additional Web addresses that pertain to the subject.

6. **Which button should Christine select to find information about "tree-free" or recycled paper?**

   Answer Ⓑ is correct. Tree-free paper is an alternative to products made from wood pulp.

7. **Where would Christine LIKELY find information about contacting her political representatives?**

   Answer Ⓒ is correct. Letter campaigns are aimed at politicians who make policy changes.

# Try It

Here is a chance to work on your prewriting and referencing skills.
Answer the questions on the next three pages.

1. It is important to use specific keywords when beginning a topic search on the Internet. What should Christine do if there are no specific links related to her topic?

_____

_____

_____

2. Understanding the major environmental issues, and the reasons why people vote a certain way, is vital when writing a persuasive essay. How could Christine do further research on her state representatives' voting patterns on environmental issues?

_____

_____

_____

3. Look at the home page options again on page 43. Which one should Christine select to find information about the giant panda?

_____

4. Here is a sample topic for research: the preservation of bald eagles. Choose the best selection of keywords to use for an Internet search on this topic.

Ⓐ raptors and bald eagles

Ⓑ preservation and eagles

Ⓒ raptors and preservation

Ⓓ bald eagles and preservation

Lesson 2: Prewriting and Referencing

5. **Knowing the difference between broad and narrow topics is important. Rank the following topics in order from narrowest (1) to broadest (4).**

    **a.**_____ politics

    **b.**_____ Campaign 2000

    **c.**_____ George W. Bush

    **d.**_____ presidential elections

6. **Which of the following keywords would narrow a search on the topic of George Washington's wife?**

    Ⓐ George Washington + politics

    Ⓑ George Washington + president

    Ⓒ George Washington + government

    Ⓓ George Washington + family life

7. **A link is a Web site that provides related information on a topic. Which of the following headings would be a logical link to the site *Save the Earth*?**

    Ⓐ Recycling

    Ⓑ Astronomy

    Ⓒ National Surf Lifesaving Association

    Ⓓ Coupons for Internet shopping

8. **Which would be the best site to check for information on how to become a forest ranger?**

    Ⓐ U.S. Army

    Ⓑ Recycling

    Ⓒ U.S. Forest Rangers Association

    Ⓓ Equal Opportunity Employment

9. What keywords could Christine use to narrow her search on recycling paper and to find information about the expenses it involves?

_____

_____

10. How could Christine find more information about endangered species other than the giant panda? What keywords could she use in her search?

_____

_____

_____

11. Which person would be most beneficial to Christine's search on paper recycling?

Ⓐ Park Ranger

Ⓑ Parent

Ⓒ Recycling Plant Manager

Ⓓ Friends

12. Organize your topics from narrowest (1) to broadest (4).

a. _____ paper recycling in the USA

b. _____ trees

c. _____ paper recycling

d. _____ paper recycling in my state

Lesson 2: Prewriting and Referencing

**Read this part of Christine's rough draft. Then answer questions 1–8.**

(1) Paper recycling is the greatest way to help save the Earth. (2) It helps protect our precious trees, and it reduces waste. (3) Recyclable paper is paper that can be recycled, recycled means that the paper has already been recycled previously. (4) Most paper has been recycled already. (5) Paper companies use their own scraps and some new paper to recycle into new paper. (6) That is not the best kind for the consumer to buy. (7) That means that no new trees were cut down to make the paper. (8) The best kind of recycled paper is 100 percent post-consumer recycled paper.

(9) There are lots of ways to help reduce the number of trees that are felled for paper. (10) Recycling cans, plastics, and glass bottles helps the Earth, too. (11) Choosing real plates and cloth napkins instead of paper ones helps reduce the waste of paper. (12) Using paper products for eating is not a good idea. (13) Recycling paper reduces the number of trees that need to be chopped down, or logged. (14) Placing used paper in recycling bins instead of the trash can helps, too. (15) We will help save, if we all make an effort to recycle and conserve paper, the Earth!

1. **Sentence 1 uses the superlative *greatest*. How should Christine rewrite the sentence so that it is more accurate?**

_____

_____

2. **How can Christine BEST separate sentence 3 into two sentences?**

_____

_____

**3. Sentence 7 is out of sequence. Which sentence would it BEST follow?**

  Ⓐ sentence 2　　　　　Ⓒ sentence 10

  Ⓑ sentence 14　　　　Ⓓ sentence 8

**4. Which sentence states the main idea of the second paragraph?**

  Ⓐ sentence 9　　　　　Ⓒ sentence 14

  Ⓑ sentence 12　　　　Ⓓ sentence 15

**5. Which sentence does NOT belong in this passage?**

  Ⓐ sentence 3　　　　　Ⓒ sentence 10

  Ⓑ sentence 8　　　　　Ⓓ sentence 12

**6. Which sentence is redundant, or not necessary?**

  Ⓐ sentence 12　　　　Ⓒ sentence 7

  Ⓑ sentence 6　　　　　Ⓓ sentence 1

**7. Sentence 13 is wordy. Rewrite the sentence to make it better. Make sure you use correct punctuation.**

_____

_____

_____

**8. Sentence 15 has faulty construction. Rewrite the sentence to make it correct.**

_____

_____

_____

## Writer's Tip

Write your reasons for your argument on separate note cards. Then you can shuffle the cards around to find the best order to present your arguments.

## Noodle Around

Superlatives are adjectives that compare two or more things in the highest degree. Which question asks you about superlatives? Discuss it with a friend.

➤ **Now check your answers. If you answered a question incorrectly, study the correct answer.**

1. **Sentence 1 uses the superlative *greatest*. How should Christine rewrite the sentence so that it is more accurate?**

   The sentence should be rewritten as follows:

   Paper recycling is a great way to help save the Earth.

2. **How can Christine BEST separate sentence 3 into two sentences?**

   The run-on sentence can BEST be separated as follows:

   Recyclable paper is paper that can be recycled. Recycled means that the paper has already been used.

3. **Sentence 7 is out of sequence. Which sentence would it BEST follow?**

   Answer Ⓓ is correct. The information describes 100 percent post-consumer recycled paper that is introduced in sentence 8.

4. **Which sentence states the main idea of the second paragraph?**

   Answer Ⓐ is the correct answer because the other sentences support it.

5. **Which sentence does NOT belong in this passage?**

   Answer Ⓒ is the correct answer. The topic of this passage relates to paper recycling.

6. **Which sentence is redundant, or not necessary?**

   Answer Ⓐ is the correct answer. Sentence 12 adds unimportant information.

7. **Sentence 13 is wordy. Rewrite the sentence to make it better.**

   Recycling paper reduces the number of trees that need to be logged.

8. **Sentence 15 has faulty construction. Rewrite the sentence to make it correct.**

   We will help save the Earth if we all make an effort to recycle and conserve paper!

# Try It

Here is a chance to work on your composing and revising skills. Answer the questions on the next three pages.

1. Writers should avoid using superlatives that cannot be supported by facts and details. Superlatives are nearly impossible to defend, so try to avoid using them. Practice changing the superlatives in these sentences.

   **a.** The stadium lights are <u>the brightest anywhere</u>.

   _____

   **b.** This is the <u>worst disaster</u>.

   _____

   **c.** Cats hate water <u>the most</u>.

   _____

2. Stating the main idea early sets the tone and topic of the whole article. Look back at the second paragraph. Can you improve upon Christine's topic sentence? Rewrite the sentence below.

   _____

   _____

   _____

3. A topic sentence states the main idea of a paragraph. Which of the following sentences would make the BEST topic sentence for a paragraph about the first day of school?

   Ⓐ I couldn't find any of my classrooms.

   Ⓑ Later, some girls helped me.

   Ⓒ I was so nervous, I didn't hear the teacher call my name.

   Ⓓ My first day of school started off as a disaster.

Lesson 3: Composing and Revising

**4.** Faulty sentence construction can confuse readers. Rewrite each sentence to improve it.

**a.** Go and hurry up to find the car.

_____

**b.** Where are you going to?

_____

**c.** I got alots of homework today.

_____

**5.** Adverbs describe action and adjectives describe objects. Circle the BEST word to complete each sentence.

**a.** My mother (quickly / quick) made my lunch.

**b.** The coach thinks (high / highly) of you.

**c.** The dog barked (ferocious / ferociously).

**6.** Make sure your sentences support your topic sentence. Which of the following sentences would not support the topic sentence, "Getting a dog was the best thing that ever happened to me"?

Ⓐ I always wanted a dog, but I didn't think my parents would let me have one.

Ⓑ Sometimes I wish I had a cat.

Ⓒ I couldn't believe it, I opened my present and out jumped a puppy!

Ⓓ They always told me that taking care of a pet was too big of a responsibility.

7. **Fix the faulty construction errors in the sentences below. Rewrite each corrected sentence on the line.**

a. Me and Jasmine are wearing brown shirts today.

_____

b. Are you coming with Jasmine and I?

_____

c. Jake and I and Seth and Mel are going to the meeting after school.

_____

8. **Separate the following sentences into two sentences without changing the meaning.**

a. We are having burgers for dinner and we are having ice cream for dessert.

_____

b. Jumping over barrels on a motorcycle is a dangerous stunt, I can't believe anyone would ever try it.

_____

c. Tomorrow is report card day for the grade school but we don't get our report cards until Monday.

_____

9. **Put the following sentences in the correct sequence using the numbers 1 to 4.**

a. _____ First, I brush my teeth.

b. _____ Then, I put on my pajamas.

c. _____ I always do my nighttime routine in the same order.

d. _____ Finally, I go to sleep.

Lesson 3: Composing and Revising

> **Read the rest of Christine's rough draft of her persuasive article. Notice the groups of underlined words. Questions 1-8 will ask about them.**

(16) Recently, the city recycling <u>service gived</u> me some information about recycling paper. (17) There <u>is many different type of paper.</u> (18) <u>Some paper they don't want</u> cause it is extremely expensive to remove stubborn inks and glues from some paper. (19) Most recycled newspapers become our daily newspapers again.

(20) Paper <u>that go</u> in the garbage goes in massive landfills. (21) A landfill is where garbage is <u>buryed</u> in the ground. (22) The ground is <u>lined so as that the garbage don't leak</u> into the city's groundwater. (23) If we don't want to fill the Earth with garbage, <u>because we should recycle more paper!</u>

1. How should Christine link the first section of her rough draft on page 48 to her second section on this page? Write a linking sentence for her.

   _____

   _____

2. How should Christine edit the underlined part of sentence 16?

   Ⓐ service give      Ⓒ service gave

   Ⓑ services gived      Ⓓ services given

3. How should Christine edit the underlined part of sentence 17?

   Ⓐ are many different type of paper.

   Ⓑ is many different type of papers.

   Ⓒ is many different types of papers.

   Ⓓ are many different types of paper.

4. **How should Christine edit the first part of sentence 18?**

   Ⓐ Recycling services don't want some paper cause

   Ⓑ Recycling services don't want some paper because

   Ⓒ It don't want some paper because

   Ⓓ They don't want some paper because

5. **How should Christine edit the underlined words in sentence 20?**

   Ⓐ that goes        Ⓒ that goed

   Ⓑ that went       Ⓓ that got

6. **How should Christine edit the underlined word in sentence 21?**

   Ⓐ bury           Ⓒ berry

   Ⓑ buried        Ⓓ berried

7. **How should Christine edit the underlined words in sentence 22?**

   Ⓐ line so that the garbage don't leak

   Ⓑ lined so as that the garbage doesn't leak

   Ⓒ lined so as that the garbages doesn't leak

   Ⓓ lined so that the garbage doesn't leak

8. **How should Christine edit the underlined part of sentence 23? Write the sentence on the line.**

   _____

   _____

   _____

## Writer's Tip

Proofreading is an important step in the writing process. After you have checked your work, ask someone else to check it for you. Sometimes, another person will see mistakes you missed.

## Noodle Around

Verbs and the subjects they relate to should agree in a sentence. If there are two or more subjects, the verb must be plural. Which question asks you about agreement? Talk it over with a friend.

Lesson 4: Editing

➤ **Now check your answers. If you answered a question incorrectly, study the correct answer.**

1. **How should Christine link the first section of her rough draft to her second section on this page?**

   Christine's introduction could read:

   As part of my effort to learn about recycling, I contacted the city recycling service.

2. **How should Christine edit the underlined part of sentence 16?**

   Answer Ⓒ is the correct answer because *gave* is the singular past tense form of the verb *give*.

3. **How should Christine edit the underlined part of sentence 17?**

   Answer Ⓓ is the correct answer because the sentence refers to more than one kind of paper. The verb *are* agrees with the plural noun *types*.

4. **How should Christine edit the first part of sentence 18?**

   Answer Ⓑ is the correct answer.

5. **How should Christine edit the underlined words in sentence 20?**

   Answer Ⓐ is the correct answer. The word *paper* is singular, so it needs the singular, present tense form of the verb *go*, which is *goes*.

6. **How should Christine edit the underlined word in sentence 21?**

   Answer Ⓑ is the correct answer. *Buried* is the correct spelling of the past tense form of the verb *bury*.

7. **How should Christine edit the underlined words in sentence 22?**

   Answer Ⓓ is the correct answer. The verb *doesn't* agrees with the singular noun *garbage*.

8. **How should Christine rewrite the underlined part of sentence 23?**

   Christine should rewrite the sentence to eliminate the word *because*:

   . . . garbage, we should recycle more paper!

# Try It

Here is a chance to work on your editing skills. Answer the questions on the next three pages.

1. Having subject-verb agreement in a sentence is important to help readers understand your writing. Correct the subject-verb agreement in the following sentences.

   **a.** The baseballs is in the bag.

   _____

   **b.** One of the best burgers are at that restaurant.

   _____

   **c.** He shoot the basket at the buzzer.

   _____

2. Here is another word that is commonly misused. Rewrite the sentence so that it is correct.

   How does the new rule <u>effect</u> you?

   _____

3. Make sure your verbs are in the same tense. Read each sentence pair. Rewrite the sentences to make the verb tense consistent.

   **a.** Did you see that catch? Yes I seen it.

   _____

   **b.** We have recycled paper for five years. We will recycled cans for five years.

   _____

   _____

## Writer's Tip

A verb in the present tense shows action that is happening now. A verb in the past tense shows action that has already happened. Make sure you use verbs in the correct tense when you write.

**4. Here is another poorly written sentence. Rewrite it to make its meaning clear.**

On account of the fire trucks needing to get through we had to move our cars.

_____

_____

**5. The following underlined words are commonly misused. Rewrite each sentence using the correct spelling.**

**a.** <u>Their</u> not coming to the party.

_____

**b.** The books are over <u>they're</u>.

_____

**c.** Did you give them <u>there</u> boxed lunches?

_____

**6. Here are some more subject-verb agreement errors. Rewrite each sentence to fix the errors.**

**a.** The books is right on the table.

_____

**b.** She don't have any books overdue at the library.

_____

**c.** Marcy do the puzzle all by herself.

_____

**7. Rewrite the following sentence to make its meaning clearer.**

There won't be any school tomorrow, supposin' it snows too much.

_____

_____

8. **Circle the subject and verb in each sentence. Find the sentences with the subject-verb agreement error. Write the correct word for each error on the line.**

   **a.** The class is going on a field trip. _____

   **b.** Justin isn't going along. _____

   **c.** The book about dinosaurs are overdue. _____

   **d.** The kids is all excited about learning to play the drums. _____

9. **Here is another poorly written sentence. Rewrite it to make its meaning clear.**

   You being late for class is a problem because everyone is waiting to take a test before you got here.

   _____

   _____

10. **Unclear writing detracts from original ideas. Rewrite the following sentence to make its meaning clearer.**

    If'n we go on vacation this year, we'll have to save our money.

    _____

    _____

11. **Editing involves reviewing word choice and correcting errors. Choose the best way to edit the following sentence.**

    The computer busted so I couldn't write my report.

    Ⓐ The computer is busted, so I couldn't write my report.
    Ⓑ The computer breaked, so I couldn't write my report.
    Ⓒ The computer broked, so I couldn't write my report.
    Ⓓ The computer broke, so I couldn't write my report.

Lesson 4: Editing

# Lesson 5  Evaluate Writing

➤ **Now you are going to read and evaluate a persuasive article that Christine wrote. The article is about the giant panda. Before you begin, read the checklist below.**

## Writing Checklist

Christine will earn her best score if she achieves the following goals:

| | |
|---|---|
| **Ideas** | • Ideas are original<br>• Topic is clearly identified<br>• Ideas support the topic |
| **Organization** | • Ideas are related and presented in correct order<br>• Strong beginning, middle, and end |
| **Creativity and Word Choice** | • Words used appropriately<br>• Creative descriptions<br>• Words enhance ideas |
| **Sentence Structure** | • Complete sentences<br>• Clearly written and easy to understand |
| **Spelling and Punctuation** | • Few or no errors |

➤ **Read the directions Christine was given.**

**Directions:** Write a persuasive article related to deforestation. Persuade your audience to agree with your point of view. Make sure your writing is organized and that you use words in their proper form.

## The Giant Pandas

(1) There are only about 1,000 left in the whole world. (2) The giant panda is one of the rarest mammals. (3) No one outside of the "Middle Kingdom," or China, was aware that they existed until the late eighteenth century. (4) They used to think that they were related to raccoons. (5) New DNA evidence confirms that giant pandas are really bears.

(6) Pandas are solitary animals. (7) They do not live with other pandas. (8) Even in zoos, or captivity, they ignore each other except when mating season begins. (9) Female pandas give birth to one or two cubs, but only care for the dominant, healthy cub. (10) The other one is rejected and died. (11) This is one of the reasons that there population is so low.

(12) The giant panda is a precious, endangered animal. (13) We have to protect them and their habitat for them to survive into the next century! (14) Scientists agree with me that we need to make big changes to save them. (15) Giant manatees are also endangered. (16) They will probably become extinct, or die out, within the next 100 years if we don't do something! (17) The main threat to the panda is the destruction of its natural habitat. (18) The population of China is growing the people need more room to live and they need to raise crops and animals. (19) The panda's natural bamboo forests are quickly disappearing because of deforestation.

Lesson 5: Evaluate Writing

(20) The United States is attempting to help the pandas, too, but we are not doing enough! (21) In 1984, the U.S. Fish and Wildlife Service listed the giant panda as an endangered species under the Endangered Species Act. (22) This prevents anyone from importing pandas to the United States without special permission.

(23) The Chinese government is trying to protect the pandas, but I think they should do more! (24) They have made eleven areas where bamboo grows, called natural preserves, for pandas to live. (25) No people is allowed to live on the preserves. (26) Only a few people are even allowed to enter them. (27) If the Chinese government catches someone killing, or poaching, a panda for its fur, that person is sentenced to life in prison!

(28) We need to save the pandas! (29) There are many reasons these gentle animals deserve our help. (30) First, they play a role in the animal kingdom. (31) They help to keep the Earth's ecology in balance. (32) We do not know what the consequences might be if they were eliminated from the animal world. (33) Third, another reason we should protect them is that we can learn more about them. (34) Scientists have only known about them for about 100 years, and it would be tragic if they disappeared so soon. (35) Once an animal is extinct, there is no way to bring it back. (36) We have to raise money to save them!

**Now answer the following questions about Christine's article.**

1. Sentence 2 is not in the correct sequence. Which one of the sentences would it BEST precede?

   Ⓐ sentence 1      Ⓒ sentence 5

   Ⓑ sentence 4      Ⓓ sentence 6

2. Sentence 4 is written poorly. Rewrite the sentence using proper usage.

   _____

   _____

3. The second paragraph does not have a topic sentence. Write one on the lines below.

   _____

   _____

4. Sentence 10 uses a word incorrectly. How would you edit the word?

   Ⓐ die      Ⓒ dies

   Ⓑ dead      Ⓓ death

5. Sentence 11 uses a word incorrectly. How would you edit the word?

   Ⓐ they're      Ⓒ their

   Ⓑ they are      Ⓓ theyr'e

## Writer's Tip

A topic sentence states the main idea of a paragraph. Any information that follows should support the topic sentence.

6. **Sentence 18 is written incorrectly. Rewrite the sentence using proper usage.**

_____

_____

7. **Sentence 25 is written incorrectly. Rewrite the sentence using proper usage.**

_____

_____

8. **Which sentence does not belong in this article?**

   Ⓐ sentence 12          Ⓒ sentence 22

   Ⓑ sentence 15          Ⓓ sentence 27

9. **The paragraph that begins with sentence 20 is out of sequence. Which paragraph should it follow?**

   Ⓐ The paragraph that begins with sentence 6.

   Ⓑ The paragraph that begins with sentence 23.

   Ⓒ The paragraph is in the correct sequence.

   Ⓓ The paragraph should be deleted.

10. **Sentence 33 has faulty construction. Rewrite it using proper construction.**

_____

_____

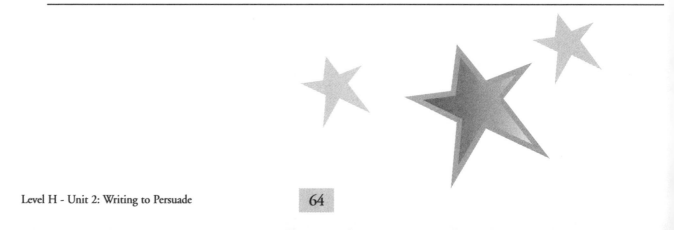

11. **Christine's article does not have a proper introduction. Write an introductory paragraph that will make her article score higher.**

_____

_____

_____

_____

_____

_____

_____

## Writer's Tip

Persuasive articles depend on a strong introduction to state the writer's opinion, or an argument. Review your introductory paragraph to be sure it clearly states your opinion.

12. **Christine states that money is needed to help the pandas survive, but she does not support this statement with examples of how the money would help. Rewrite the paragraph to add the necessary information to support the statement.**

_____

_____

_____

_____

_____

_____

13. **Did Christine stick to her essay topic throughout this piece? Explain your answer.**

_____

_____

_____

_____

# Evaluate Christine's Writing

➤ **Here is a guide for evaluating writing called a rubric. Rubrics are used to grade tests. Use this rubric to rate Christine's article.**

# Writing Rubric

| Score | Ideas | Organization | Creativity and Word Choice | Sentence Structure | Spelling and Punctuation |
|---|---|---|---|---|---|
| 4 | • Ideas are original<br>• Topic is clearly identified<br>• Ideas support the topic | • Ideas are related and presented in correct order<br>• Strong beginning, middle, and end | • Words used appropriately<br>• Creative descriptions<br>• Words enhance ideas | • Complete sentences<br>• Clearly written and easy to understand | • Few or no errors |
| 3 | • Some ideas are original<br>• Most ideas support the topic | • Most ideas are related and presented in correct order<br>• Good beginning, middle, and end | • Most words used appropriately<br>• Some creative descriptions<br>• Words support ideas | • Many sentences are complete<br>• Most sentences are clearly written and easy to understand | • Some errors |
| 2 | • Few ideas are original<br>• Ideas wander from topic<br>• Some details support the topic | • Some ideas are related and presented in correct order<br>• Weak beginning, middle, and end | • Some words used appropriately<br>• Few creative descriptions | • Some run-on or fragmented sentences<br>• Some sentences are unclear | • Many errors |
| 1 | • Ideas are incomplete<br>• Few details support the topic | • Few ideas are related and presented in correct order<br>• No real beginning, middle, and end | • Few words used appropriately<br>• No attempt at creative descriptions | • Several run-on or fragmented sentences<br>• Many sentences are unclear | • Serious errors |
| 0 | • No attempt | • No attempt | • No attempt | • No attempt | • No attempt |

➤ **Give Christine's writing a score of 0 to 4 for each category. Explain why you gave her that score.**

☐ **Ideas** _____
score
_____
_____
_____

☐ **Organization** _____
score
_____
_____
_____

☐ **Creativity and Word Choice** _____
score
_____
_____
_____

☐ **Sentence Structure** _____
score
_____
_____
_____

☐ **Spelling and Punctuation** _____
score
_____
_____

Lesson 5: Evaluate Writing

# Lesson 6 Your Turn to Write

➤ **Now it is your turn to write about a specific topic. Read the directions below. Then read the checklist that you and your teacher will use to evaluate your writing.**

**Directions:** Choose an animal that is endangered due to deforestation. Write an article that persuades readers to save this endangered species. List the causes of its threatened state and provide a summary of information about the animal. Be sure your persuasion is well organized. Remember to schedule enough time to find the information you will need to fully research your topic.

## Writing Checklist

I will earn my best score if I achieve the following goals:

| | |
|---|---|
| **Ideas** | • Ideas are original<br>• Topic is clearly identified<br>• Ideas support the topic |
| **Organization** | • Ideas are related and presented in correct order<br>• Strong beginning, middle, and end |
| **Creativity and Word Choice** | • Words used appropriately<br>• Creative descriptions<br>• Words enhance ideas |
| **Sentence Structure** | • Complete sentences<br>• Clearly written and easy to understand |
| **Spelling and Punctuation** | • Few or no errors |

# Plan Your Writing

➤ **Use these pages to plan your writing. You may find this graphic organizer helpful.**

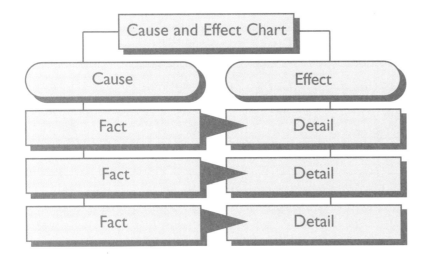

**Writer's Tip**

When writing a persuasive article, be sure to support your ideas with facts and details.

_____

_____

_____

_____

_____

_____

_____

_____

_____

_____

_____

_____

_____

Lesson 6: Your Turn to Write

# Plan Your Writing

---

## Writer's Tip

Good writers guide their readers through the piece of writing. Insert sentences that tell readers where your argument is heading. This can take the form of stating the number of reasons you will present.

## Writer's Tip

Think carefully about who will read your article. What will your reader need to understand difficult terms?

## Writer's Tip

Avoid using superlatives. They are difficult to defend or prove. Use keywords like *almost* or *nearly always* to soften a superlative.

# Write Your Final Draft

▶ **Use all the skills you have learned in this unit to score well on your final draft. Remember to carefully proofread your work before giving it to your teacher.**

1 _____

2 _____

3 _____

4 _____

5 _____

6 _____

7 _____

8 _____

9 _____

10 _____

11 _____

12 _____

13 _____

14 _____

15 _____

16 _____

17 _____

18 _____

19 _____

20 _____

21 _____

22 _____

23 _____

24 _____

25 _____

26 _____

27 _____

28 _____

29 _____

30 _____

31 _____

32 _____

33 _____

34 _____

35 _____

36 _____

37 _____

38 _____

39 _____

40 _____

41 _____

42 _____

43 _____

44 _____

45 _____

Lesson 6: Your Turn to Write

# Evaluate Your Writing

➤ **Here is the same rubric you used to evaluate Christine's writing. Use it to evaluate your writing.**

# Writing Rubric

| Score | Ideas | Organization | Creativity and Word Choice | Sentence Structure | Spelling and Punctuation |
|---|---|---|---|---|---|
| **4** | • Ideas are original<br>• Topic is clearly identified<br>• Ideas support the topic | • Ideas are related and presented in correct order<br>• Strong beginning, middle, and end | • Words used appropriately<br>• Creative descriptions<br>• Words enhance ideas | • Complete sentences<br>• Clearly written and easy to understand | • Few or no errors |
| **3** | • Some ideas are original<br>• Most ideas support the topic | • Most ideas are related and presented in correct order<br>• Good beginning, middle, and end | • Most words used appropriately<br>• Some creative descriptions<br>• Words support ideas | • Many sentences are complete<br>• Most sentences are clearly written and easy to understand | • Some errors |
| **2** | • Few ideas are original<br>• Ideas wander from topic<br>• Some details support the topic | • Some ideas are related and presented in correct order<br>• Weak beginning, middle, and end | • Some words used appropriately<br>• Few creative descriptions | • Some run-on or fragmented sentences<br>• Some sentences are unclear | • Many errors |
| **1** | • Ideas are incomplete<br>• Few details support the topic | • Few ideas are related and presented in correct order<br>• No real beginning, middle, and end | • Few words used appropriately<br>• No attempt at creative descriptions | • Several run-on or fragmented sentences<br>• Many sentences are unclear | • Serious errors |
| **0** | • No attempt | • No attempt | • No attempt | • No attempt | • No attempt |

➤ **Give your own writing a score of 0 to 4 for each category. Explain why you gave yourself that score.**

[  ]
score
Ideas _____
_____
_____
_____

[  ]
score
Organization _____
_____
_____
_____

[  ]
score
Creativity and Word Choice _____
_____
_____
_____

[  ]
score
Sentence Structure _____
_____
_____
_____

[  ]
score
Spelling and Punctuation _____
_____
_____

Lesson 6: Your Turn to Write

➤ **Does the glory of Olympic gold appeal to you? On the lines below, write down some things you know about your favorite Olympic sport. Then read the article that follows.**

_____

_____

_____

# The Making of the Modern Olympics

Inspired by the Ancient Olympics, the Modern Olympic Games have established a rich tradition of their own. However, today's Olympics are quite different from the Ancient Olympics that began in 776 B.C.

The original contests were held every four years as a religious festival in Greece at a place called Olympia. Athletes trained for ten months there. While they trained, a panel of ten judges evaluated them according to their parentage, or family history; their character; and their physical traits. The judges chose only the elite athletes to compete in the games. Although the judging criteria have changed, modern athletes must still qualify to participate in each Olympic event.

_The Greek god Hercules_

For the first fifty years, there was only one event in the Ancient Olympic Games. It was called the *stade*. The stade was a running race that went the length of the stadium. The length was based on a legend that the Greek god Hercules could run this distance in one breath. Of course, there were no stopwatches or accurate ways of recording lengths of time in ancient Greece. The competition had a new winner, or titleholder, at each Ancient Olympics. There were no records to break but, legends grew about athletes who were faster than various animals, such as a hare or a horse.

Another major difference between the old and the new Olympics is the participation of women. In ancient Greece, women were forbidden to participate or even attend the Olympic events. In fact, the punishment for such an offense was death. Instead, they started their own version of the games, called the Heraea Games. Like the men's Olympics, they were held every four years.

Even though women were excluded from the Ancient Olympics, they were often declared winners of events. How? In horse racing and charioteering events, the winner of the event was the owner of the horse! Many rich women owned horses and chariots. They hired men to ride their horses or drive the chariots. Many wealthy women often won a race that they could neither compete in nor attend.

The Ancient Olympics continued until A.D. 400, when Gauth marauders destroyed the shrine to Olympia. It was not until 1896 that the Modern Olympics were reestablished in Athens, Greece. A Frenchman, Baron Pierre de Coubertin, came up with the idea.

Many traditions of the Modern Olympics have developed over the years, including the swearing of the Olympic oath, the burning of the torch, the releasing of the doves at the opening ceremonies, and the awarding of gold, silver, and bronze medals. Many changes have been made since the original olive branches were awarded to Olympians in ancient Greece, but the concept that the Olympics is the ultimate athletic proving ground remains the same.

*Baron Pierre de Coubertin*

▶ **Damion's class was studying the Olympics. They were asked to write a factual report about a modern Olympic event. Damion was interested in the heptathlon.**

**To help him decide what he needed to know, Damion searched a Web site using the search word *heptathlon*. Read the list of related sites that he found in his search and use it to answer questions 1–3.**

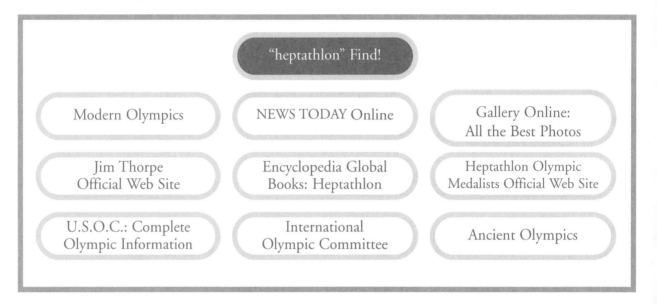

1. **Which of the Web sites would be a good place to find pictures of recent heptathlon event**

   Ⓐ Encyclopedia Global Books: Heptathlon    Ⓒ Gallery Online: All the Best Photos

   Ⓑ Jim Thorpe Official Web Site    Ⓓ Ancient Olympics

2. **Which of the Web sites would NOT be a good place to search for information about the origins of the heptathlon?**

   Ⓐ Modern Olympics    Ⓒ Encyclopedia Global Books: Heptathlon

   Ⓑ Ancient Olympics    Ⓓ U.S.O.C.: Complete Olympic Information

3. **Which Web site would be the BEST place to find information about Jackie Joyner-Kersee, a recent Olympic gold medalist?**

   Ⓐ International Olympic Committee

   Ⓑ Heptathlon Olympic Medalists Official Web Site

   Ⓒ Jim Thorpe Official Web Site

   Ⓓ Ancient Olympics

➤ **Here is a list of category headings for the Web site *Encyclopedia Global Books: heptathlon*. Use it to answer questions 4–7.**

- **HISTORY**
- **MEETS/STATISTICS**
- **EVENTS:**
    - RUNNING
    - HURDLING
    - RELAYS
    - WALKING
    - JUMPING
    - THROWING
    - DECATHLON AND HEPTATHLON
- **ATHLETES**

## Writer's Tip

Keywords are very important when searching the Web. Some words have more than one meaning. For example, a search for *George Washington* will bring up sites that relate to both the president and the university. Searching for *George Washington, president,* will steer you away from the university sites.

4. **Which heading should Damion select to find information on the height and spacing of the hurdles?**

    (A) History       (C) Events: Hurdling

    (B) Events: Throwing       (D) Meets/Stats

5. **Which heading should Damion select to find information on Jackie Joyner-Kersee?**

    (A) History       (C) Events: Decathlon and Heptathlon

    (B) Meets/Stats       (D) Athletes

6. **Which heading would be the BEST site for statistical information about race results?**

    (A) History       (C) Events: Walking

    (B) Meets/Stats       (D) Events: Jumping

7. **How would Damion find additional information about Jackie Joyner-Kersee's development as an athlete?**

_____

_____

## Noodle Around

When writers organize and research their ideas, they search for statistics or facts to explain their main idea. Which question asks you about statistics? Discuss it with a friend.

➤ **Now check your answers. If you answered a question incorrectly, study the correct answer.**

1. **Which of the Web sites would be a good place to find pictures of recent heptathlon events?**

   Answer Ⓒ is the correct answer. The word *gallery* means a collection of items.

2. **Which of the Web sites would NOT be a good place to search for information about the origins of the heptathlon?**

   Answer Ⓐ is the correct answer. This news site would feature recent or upcoming events.

3. **Which Web site would be the BEST place to find information about Jackie Joyner-Kersee a recent Olympic gold medalist?**

   Answer Ⓑ is the correct answer. Jackie Joyner-Kersee is a modern medalist.

4. **Which heading should Damion select to find information on the height and spacing of the hurdles?**

   Answer Ⓒ is the correct answer. Information about the hurdling event would be found under its specific event heading.

5. **Which heading should Damion select to find information on Jackie Joyner-Kersee?**

   Answer Ⓓ is the correct answer. Although Joyner-Kersee may be featured under the other headings, the main information would be under *Athletes*.

6. **Which heading would be the BEST site for statistical information about race results?**

   Answer Ⓑ is the correct answer. Statistical information and race results would fall under the category of *Meets/Stats*.

7. **How would Damion find additional information about Jackie Joyner-Kersee's development as an athlete?**

   Damion could find further information about Joyner-Kersee by selecting a link on the Web site after finding her under the heading *Athletes*. Damion could also check the library for reference books, biographies, and books on sports.

## Try It

> **Here is a chance to work on your prewriting and referencing skills. Answer the questions on the next three pages.**

1. Retracing your search path helps you see if you strayed off the topic. Review Damion's initial search on page 78 again. Which headings would Damion select to find information on the following?

    **a.** Olympic qualifiers for 2000 _____

    **b.** Regulations for the walking competition _____

    **c.** World record holders _____

2. Jackie Joyner-Kersee's sister-in-law, Florence Griffith Joyner, was also an Olympic athlete. How can Damion find information about her?

    _____

    _____

3. Use specific keywords when beginning a search. Narrow the following topics to avoid confusion during your Internet search.

    **a.** Paul Bunyan's legends in Minnesota

    _____

    _____

    **b.** Michael Jordan's baseball career

    _____

    _____

    **c.** John Glenn's service in the U.S. Senate

    _____

    _____

*Jackie Joyner-Kersee*

Lesson 2: Prewriting and Referencing

4. **If Damion wants to switch his topic to Florence Griffith Joyner's medals, how would he find information about them? What keywords could he use?**

_____

_____

5. **To narrow a Web search, use specific keywords. Which of the following keywords would provide the best search on the topic of Olympic records?**

Ⓐ records

Ⓑ Olympics + records

Ⓒ Olympics + gold medals

Ⓓ world records

6. **How could Damion find more information about Jackie Joyner-Kersee's community service? What keywords could he use?**

_____

_____

7. **Which of the following keywords would be BEST for finding information about the first Olympic games?**

Ⓐ Modern Olympics

Ⓑ Ancient Olympics

Ⓒ International Olympic Committee

Ⓓ U.S.O.C.: Complete Olympic Information

8. **How could Damion find more information about Jackie Joyner-Kersee's asthmatic condition? What keywords could he use?**

_____

_____

9. **Which link would provide information about how young athletes cope with asthma?**

   (A) Jackie Joyner-Kersee

   (B) high school sports

   (C) teen talk

   (D) asthma and athletics

10. **Sometimes you will find that a link does not give you the information you want. What would be the best way to get back on track with your search?**

    (A) select the "back" icon

    (B) select the "disconnect" icon

    (C) begin a new search

    (D) select the "forward" icon

11. **Topic webs are another way to discover what kinds of details are missing as you conduct research. Which idea could be added to Damion's topic web?**

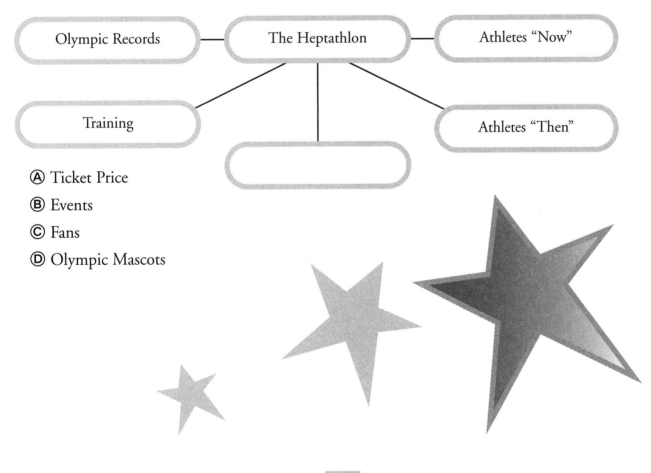

   (A) Ticket Price

   (B) Events

   (C) Fans

   (D) Olympic Mascots

Lesson 2: Prewriting and Referencing

**Read this part of Damion's rough draft. Then answer questions 1–7.**

(1) The heptathlon is a modern women's event that is part of the "Athletics," or track and field events of the Olympic games. (2) Seven events compose the modern women's heptathlon. (3) These events require a two-day competition to complete the heptathlon. (4) The seven elements of the event are the 100-meter hurdles, high jump, shot put, 200-meter dash, long jump, javelin throw, and 800-meter race. (5) Athletes are awarded points for placing in each event. (6) Each event has points that are awarded to the successful athletes. (7) The athletes are awarded points for each event.

(8) The running segments makes up nearly half of the event. (9) The 100-meter hurdles require speed and agility. (10) The runner sprints and jumps over obstacles, called hurdles. (11) A hurdler is allowed to knock down the hurdle without being disqualified. (12) It must really hurt to bang your shins on it though! (13) However, she must not touch the hurdle with her hands or move out of her lane to avoid it. (14) The goal is to establish a smooth running rhythm that will result in the fastest time. (15) Then the 200-meter dash, which is considered a sprint. (16) The 800-meter race is a middle-distance race that requires pacing and sprinting.

(17) The field events of the heptathlon are the high jump, long jump, shot put, and javelin toss. (18) Each field event requires strength and speed and agility. (19) These events generally take place within the oval of the running track or nearby it.

1.  **Combine sentences 2 and 3 to make a more complex sentence without changing the meaning.**

    _____

    _____

**2. Which sentence is redundant, or repeats information?**

(A) sentence 7      (C) sentence 2

(B) sentence 10      (D) sentence 4

**3. Sentence 8 is poorly written. Rewrite the sentence to make it correct.**

_____

_____

**4. Which sentence does NOT belong in this passage?**

(A) sentence 4      (C) sentence 12

(B) sentence 11      (D) sentence 16

**5. Damion's main objective in this draft is to—**

(A) persuade the reader.      (C) entertain.

(B) explain and inform.      (D) reflect on personal feelings.

**6. Which paragraph states the main idea?**

(A) first      (C) third

(B) second      (D) none

**7. Sentence 18 is poorly written. Rewrite it to improve the structure.**

_____

_____

Writer's Tip

Use transition words to link ideas in your writing. Transition words help readers follow your train of thought.

Noodle Around

Writers use list, or serial, commas to separate a number of items in a list. Which question asks you about the use of serial commas? Discuss it with a friend.

Lesson 3: Composing and Revising

## Composing and Revising

➤ **Now check your answers. If you answered a question incorrectly, study the correct answer.**

1. **Combine sentences 2 and 3 to make a more complex sentence without changing the meaning.**

   Your answer should not change the meaning of the sentence. For example:

   Seven events compose the modern women's heptathlon, which requires a two-day competition.

2. **Which sentence is redundant, or not necessary?**

   Answer Ⓐ is the correct answer. This sentence is not needed because the previous sentence states that points are awarded.

3. **Sentence 8 is poorly written. Rewrite the sentence to make it correct.**

   Your answer should not change the meaning of the sentence. For example:

   The running segments compose nearly half of the event.

4. **Which sentence does NOT belong in this passage?**

   Answer Ⓒ is correct. The assignment is to write a factual report. There is no need for personal opinion.

5. **Damion's main objective in this draft is to—**

   The correct answer is Ⓑ explain and inform.

6. **Which paragraph states the main idea?**

   The correct answer is Ⓐ. The main idea is stated in the first paragraph. The other paragraphs state supporting details.

7. **Sentence 18 is poorly written. Rewrite it to improve the structure.**

   Repeating the word *and* in a sentence is awkward. Commas should be inserted for all but the last item in the sequence. The sentence should be rewritten as follows:

   Each field event requires strength, speed, and agility.

# Try It

> **Here is a chance to work on your composing and revising skills. Answer the questions on the next three pages.**

1. **Redundant information distracts the reader. Here are three sets of sentences. Circle the words that present redundant information.**

    **a.** The boy is wearing a green shirt and hat. He is also wearing a green hat.

    **b.** Jericho had spaghetti for lunch. Spaghetti was what Jericho chose for lunch.

    **c.** The movie was thrilling. I loved the part in the movie with the space ships.

2. **By not finishing the ideas, incomplete sentences can leave the reader hanging. Rewrite each incomplete sentence to make it complete.**

    **a.** If you would buy the shoes.

    _____

    **b.** Are you going to?

    _____

    **c.** Since they are on sale.

    _____

3. **Short sentences can break a reader's rhythm. The following sentences would sound better combined. Rewrite each set as one complete sentence.**

    **a.** I'm hungry. I want food now.

    _____

    **b.** Playing with the beach ball was fun. The beach ball got a hole in it.

    _____

    **c.** My homework is done. I am going outside now.

    _____

Lesson 3: Composing and Revising

**4.** The following sentence is poorly written. It has a usage error and its meaning is unclear. Rewrite the sentence to improve it.

I sort of understood what Mr. Thomson was asking me to do.

_____

**5.** Sentence fragments also leave your reader hanging. Which of the following sentences is incomplete?

(A) But we never found out.

(B) Go over there.

(C) Where is it?

(D) You don't know either.

**6.** Which set of sentences presents redundant information? Circle the sentences that are redundant.

**a.** The oven is hot. The oven is very hot.

**b.** This book is very exciting. It is the best thriller I've ever read.

**c.** School was released early today. We went home before the usual time.

**d.** The dog's hair is gray. It looks very old.

**7.** Here are some more sentence fragments. Rewrite the following sentences to make them complete.

**a.** But there weren't any cookies left.

_____

**b.** If you want to find out more.

_____

**c.** Just because it was raining.

_____

8. **Combine the following sentences to make a more complex sentence without changing its meaning.**

The fireworks were the best I've ever seen. The fireworks display was spectacular.

_____

9. **There is a difference between stating an opinion and presenting a fact. Which of the following sentences is an opinion?**

Ⓐ We must do something about the landfill problem.

Ⓑ Landfills are a growing concern in our community.

Ⓒ Do you know where your garbage goes?

Ⓓ It makes me upset to think about landfills.

10. **Opinions are often written in the first-person voice. Label each of the following sentences as first-, second-, or third-person voice.**

a. I believe that the time has come for a real change. _____

b. Lisa looked out the window. _____

c. Baseball is my favorite sport. _____

11. **Complete the following statement. The main objective of a report is to—**

Ⓐ inform the reader.

Ⓑ entertain the reader.

Ⓒ convince the reader.

Ⓓ confuse the reader.

## Writer's Tip

Check that your writing maintains the same voice. Switching from first- to third-person voice can distract readers.

# Lesson 4 — Editing

▶ **Read the rest of Damion's rough draft of his report. Notice the groups of underlined words. Questions 1–8 will ask about them.**

(20) The <u>high jump is a contest</u> of great height and strength. (21) The <u>jumper hasta leave the ground</u> on one foot, not two. (22) Then she must clear a thin bar in one jump. (23) If she fails in her first attempt, she can continue to try to clear the bar until she misses three consecetive times. (24) Originally, athletes landed in a sand or dirt pit. (25) Modern events have inflated foam or rubber pits for a softer landing. (26) This has reduced the number of shoulder and neck injuries suffered by athletes in the event.

(27) The long jump is a contest of distance and speed. (28) It was formerly called <u>the broad jump and speed is essential</u> in this event. (29) Athletes leave the ground with a one-foot takeoff from a <u>board on the ground; long jumpers</u> generally use a technique that looks like they are walking through the air.

(30) The two <u>tossing events is the shot put</u> and the javelin throw. (31) The shot put, in the women's event, requires the athletes to push an <u>8-pound 13-ounce metal ball</u>. (32) <u>The ball was basically pushed through the air.</u> (33) The javelin is a lightweight spearlike stick that the athletes hurl over the shoulder at the end of a short sprint. (34) These events require a great deal of weight training to build up strength and endurance.

1. **How should Damion edit the underlined part of sentence 20?**

   Ⓐ High Jump is a contest
   Ⓑ High jump is a contest
   Ⓒ high jump is a Contest
   Ⓓ correct as it is

2. **How should Damion edit the underlined part of sentence 21?**

   Ⓐ jumper gots to leave the ground
   Ⓑ jumper can't leave the ground
   Ⓒ jumper must leave the ground
   Ⓓ correct as it is

3. **Find the spelling error in sentence 23. Which item spells the word correctly?**

Ⓐ continue

Ⓑ clear

Ⓒ till

Ⓓ consecutive

4. **How should Damion edit the underlined part of sentence 28?**

Ⓐ the broad, jump and speed is essential

Ⓒ the broad jump, and speed is essential

Ⓑ the broad jump and, speed is essential

Ⓓ no changes needed

5. **How should Damion edit the underlined part of sentence 29?**

Ⓐ board on the ground, long jumpers

Ⓑ board, on the ground, long jumpers

Ⓒ board on the ground; long jumpers

Ⓓ board on the ground. Long jumpers

6. **How should Damion edit the underlined part of sentence 30?**

_____

_____

7. **How should Damion edit the underlined part of sentence 31?**

_____

_____

8. **Sentence 32 has improper usage. How should Damion rewrite it?**

Ⓐ The ball is basically pushed through the air.

Ⓑ The ball was basically pushing through the air.

Ⓒ The balls were basically pushed through the air.

Ⓓ The balls were basically pushing through the air.

## Writer's Tip

Before editing, take a break from your writing. A break will sometimes bring a new perspective. When you go back to it, you may find simple errors that you overlooked while writing.

Common nouns do not need to be capitalized. Common nouns refer to people or objects in general rather than by specific names. Only proper nouns need to be capitalized. Which question asks you about capitalization? Talk it over with a friend.

Lesson 4: Editing

➤ **Now check your answers. If you answered a question incorrectly, study the correct answer.**

1. **How should Damion edit the underlined part of sentence 20?**

   Answer Ⓓ is correct. There is no need for capitalization with the common nouns in their positions.

2. **How should Damion edit the underlined part of sentence 21?**

   Answer Ⓒ is the correct answer. *Hasta* is not a word. Its implied meaning in this sentence is *must*.

3. **Find the spelling error in sentence 23. Which item spells the word correctly?**

   Answer Ⓓ is the correct answer. The other words are spelled correctly in the sentence.

4. **How should Damion edit the underlined part of sentence 28?**

   Answer Ⓒ is correct. The comma is necessary to separate two clauses combined by the conjunction *and*.

5. **How should Damion edit the underlined part of sentence 29?**

   Answer Ⓓ is correct. A period is necessary to separate two unrelated clauses without a conjunction such as *and*.

6. **How should Damion edit the underlined part of sentence 30?**

   The correct way to rewrite the segment for subject-verb agreement is:

   tossing events are the shot put

7. **How should Damion edit the underlined part of sentence 31?**

   The correct way to rewrite the segment is: an 8-pound, 13-ounce metal ball.

8. **Sentence 32 contains improper usage. How should Damion rewrite it?**

   Answer Ⓐ is the correct answer. The subject, *ball,* is singular, present tense. It requires the singular, present tense verb *is pushed*.

# Try It

➤ **Here is a chance to work on your editing skills. Answer the questions on the next three pages.**

1. Incorrect usage detracts from good writing. Rewrite these poorly written sentences to make them correct.

   **a.** Jake, please took the suitcases up stairs now.

   _____

   **b.** Is that you're book?

   _____

   **c.** Were coming to the party tonight.

   _____

2. Review the use of apostrophes in your work. A missing apostrophe or one in the wrong place can change the meaning of a word. Rewrite each sentence to correct these common apostrophe errors.

   **a.** It looks like its going to rain.

   _____

   **b.** Does the dog have it's leash?

   _____

   **c.** They put Sallys' coat in the coatroom.

   _____

3. Here are some other common usage errors. Rewrite each sentence correctly.

   **a.** She think shes great.

   _____

   **b.** He know all the answers.

   _____

   **c.** We go to the school where he go.

   _____

**4.** Colloquialisms, or slang, make writing appear informal. How would you BEST edit the following sentence so it has standard usage?

Jack isn't gonna have a birthday party this year.

_____

**5.** Check your subject-verb agreement at the editing stage. Choose the correct edit for the underlined part in the following sentence without changing the meaning of the sentence.

<u>Some of us is using</u> the computers in the library to do research.

Ⓐ Some of us using        Ⓒ None of us are using

Ⓑ None of us is using       Ⓓ Some of us are using

**6.** Edit and rewrite each sentence on the lines below.

**a.** The Miller's are going to the fireworks display tonight.

_____

**b.** The books covers are ripped on the binding.

_____

**c.** Are you going to Jamies tonight?

_____

**7.** Find the misspelled words in the following sentences, and rewrite them correctly on the lines below.

**a.** Her legal gaurdian is her aunt.

_____

**b.** The mud stuck to his work boots looked grosse.

_____

**c.** The newstand had all of the latest magazines.

_____

8. **Find the usage errors in the following sentences and rewrite each sentence correctly on the lines below.**

   **a.** The baby been crying all morning.

   _____

   **b.** We didn't never lose our power in the storm.

   _____

   **c.** The team gots six new members this season.

   _____

9. **The following sentences have either a spelling error or an apostrophe error. Rewrite each sentence correctly on the lines below.**

   **a.** My bike's tire has a whole in it.

   _____

   **b.** At school, Jeremy's computers' always having system errors.

   _____

   **c.** My grandma's chocolate chip cookies are grate!

   _____

10. **Edit the following sentence. Look for spelling, apostrophe, and usage errors. Rewrite it correctly on the lines below.**

   Maries' backpack busted open and all of her notebooks is dropping down the halway's.

   _____

   _____

Lesson 4: Editing

▶ **Now you are going to read and evaluate another article that Damion wrote. The article is about Jackie Joyner-Kersee, an Olympic gold medalist in the heptathlon event. Before you begin, read the checklist below.**

## Writing Checklist

Damion will earn his best score if he achieves the following goals:

| | |
|---|---|
| **Ideas** | • Ideas are original<br>• Topic is clearly identified<br>• Ideas support the topic |
| **Organization** | • Ideas are related and presented in correct order<br>• Strong beginning, middle, and end |
| **Creativity and Word Choice** | • Words used appropriately<br>• Creative descriptions<br>• Words enhance ideas |
| **Sentence Structure** | • Complete sentences<br>• Clearly written and easy to understand |
| **Spelling and Punctuation** | • Few or no errors |

> **Read the directions Damion was given.**

**Directions:** Write an informative article about an Olympic athlete in an event that is of interest to you. Make sure your writing is organized and you use words in their proper form.

## Jackie Joyner-Kersee

(1) She was the first American woman to set a world record in a multi-event competition. (2) Jackie Joyner-Kersee is probably the greatest female athlete of all time. (3) She was also the first to break the 7,000-point barrier in the heptathlon event at the 1986 goodwill games in Moscow. (4) She won gold medals in the 1988 and 1992 Olympics. (5) She has earned many honors and awards.

*Jackie Joyner-Kersee at the 1992 Olympics held in Barcelona, Spain*

(6) Joyner-Kersee hurdled many obstacles on her way to the top. (7) One of the biggest obstacles was her "exercise-induced" asthma. (8) She managed her condition carefully. (9) She did not let it stop her from competing in athletics. (10) She earned a track scholarship to the University of California–Los Angeles.

(11) Joyner-Kersee also rose above financial strain. (12) She gives the local community center in East St. Louis Illinois, the credit for her success. (13) Joyner-Kersee attended classes and competed in many sports at the center. (14) It helped her to feel good about herself.

(15) Joyner-Kersee began running her first races at the age of 9. (16) She won four National Junior Pentathlon championships. (17) The first one was when she was 14. (18) This inspired her brother, Al, to train, too. (19) Al married Florence Griffith. (20) Al and Jackie later competed together in the Olympics.

97

(21) During college Joyner-Kersee sets her goal to compete in the Olympics. (22) One of her basketball coaches, Bob Kersee, recognizes her potential. (23) The university gives him special permission to coach her for the Olympics and later, Joyner marries her coach.

(24) When Joyner-Kersee was in high school, she competed in volleyball, basketball, and track. (25) She was not the best athlete at first. (26) Sometimes other kids teased her for being a tomboy. (27) She didn't let it bother her. (28) When she was a junior, she set the Illinois state high school girls' long jump record at 20 ft., 7.5 inches. (29) She trained hard and studied in school. (30) She graduated in the top 10 percent of her high school class.

*Jackie Joyner-Kersee with gold medal*

(31) Joyner-Kersee earned a silver medal in the heptathlon event of the Olympics in 1984 even though she had a pulled hamstring. (32) In Joyner-Kersee established herself as the greatest heptathlete in the world at the Goodwill Games in Moscow. (33) She set a new world record in the event of 7,148 points. (34) She continued to set world record's with her fourth record at the 1988 Olympics in Seoul, Korea. (35) In 1992, she became the first heptathlete to win consecutive gold Olympic medals in Barcelona, Spain. (36) Although she competed in the 1996 Olympics in Atlanta she tore another hamstring. (37) This time she earned a Bronze medal in the long jump, but had to drop out of the heptathlon because of her injury.

**Now answer the following questions about Damion's article.**

1. Sentence 2 is out of order. Which one of the sentences would it BEST precede?

   Ⓐ sentence 1          Ⓒ sentence 4

   Ⓑ sentence 3          Ⓓ sentence 5

2. Sentence 3 has capitalization errors in it. Rewrite the sentence using proper capitalization.

   _____

   _____

3. Sentences 7 and 8 tell us about Jackie's asthma. How could Damion better explain how she managed this disease?

   _____

   _____

4. Sentence 11 does not link well to the rest of the paragraph. Rewrite the sentence so that it better introduces the topic of the paragraph.

   _____

   _____

   _____

5. Sentence 12 has a punctuation error in it. Rewrite the sentence using proper punctuation.

   _____

   _____

Lesson 5: Evaluate Writing

**6. Which sentence presents material that is not related to the topic?**

Ⓐ sentence 6

Ⓒ sentence 19

Ⓑ sentence 15

Ⓓ sentence 34

**7. The paragraph that begins with sentence 21 has a change of verb tense that is not consistent with the rest of the article. Make the necessary changes on the lines below.**

_____

_____

_____

_____

**8. The paragraph that begins with sentence 21 is out of order. Which paragraph would it BEST follow? The paragraph that begins with—**

Ⓐ sentence 1.

Ⓒ sentence 24.

Ⓑ sentence 15.

Ⓓ sentence 31.

**9. Sentence 23 is a run-on sentence. Correct the sentence using proper punctuation.**

_____

_____

10. Sentence 34 has a usage error. Rewrite the sentence using proper punctuation.

_____

_____

11. Sentence 36 has a punctuation error. Rewrite the sentence using proper punctuation.

_____

_____

12. There is a capitalization error in sentence 37. How should it be edited?

Ⓐ Medal

Ⓑ Long

Ⓒ Long Jump

Ⓓ bronze

13. Damion's article does not have a clear conclusion that makes a statement or summarizes the information presented in his article. Write a conclusion that will improve his score.

_____

_____

_____

_____

_____

_____

_____

_____

_____

## Writer's Tip

A run-on sentence is two or more clauses strung together without proper punctuation. Run-on sentences make writing confusing and hard to follow. Be sure to punctuate correctly and avoid run-on sentences that distract the reader.

Lesson 5: Evaluate Writing

# Evaluate Damion's Writing

➤ **Here is a guide for evaluating writing called a rubric. Rubrics are used to grade tests. Use this rubric to rate Damion's article.**

# Writing Rubric

| Score | Ideas | Organization | Creativity and Word Choice | Sentence Structure | Spelling and Punctuation |
|---|---|---|---|---|---|
| **4** | • Ideas are original<br>• Topic is clearly identified<br>• Ideas support the topic | • Ideas are related and presented in correct order<br>• Strong beginning, middle, and end | • Words used appropriately<br>• Creative descriptions<br>• Words enhance ideas | • Complete sentences<br>• Clearly written and easy to understand | • Few or no errors |
| **3** | • Some ideas are original<br>• Most ideas support the topic | • Most ideas are related and presented in correct order<br>• Good beginning, middle, and end | • Most words used appropriately<br>• Some creative descriptions<br>• Words support ideas | • Many sentences are complete<br>• Most sentences are clearly written and easy to understand | • Some errors |
| **2** | • Few ideas are original<br>• Ideas wander from topic<br>• Some details support the topic | • Some ideas are related and presented in correct order<br>• Weak beginning, middle, and end | • Some words used appropriately<br>• Few creative descriptions | • Some run-on or fragmented sentences<br>• Some sentences are unclear | • Many errors |
| **1** | • Ideas are incomplete<br>• Few details support the topic | • Few ideas are related and presented in correct order<br>• No real beginning, middle, and end | • Few words used appropriately<br>• No attempt at creative descriptions | • Several run-on or fragmented sentences<br>• Many sentences are unclear | • Serious errors |
| **0** | • No attempt | • No attempt | • No attempt | • No attempt | • No attempt |

➤ **Give Damion's writing a score of 0 to 4 for each category. Explain why you gave him that score.**

[ ] score   Ideas _____

_____

_____

_____

[ ] score   Organization _____

_____

_____

_____

[ ] score   Creativity and Word Choice _____

_____

_____

_____

[ ] score   Sentence Structure _____

_____

_____

_____

[ ] score   Spelling and Punctuation _____

_____

_____

Lesson 5: Evaluate Writing

➤ **Now it is your turn to write about a specific topic. Read the directions below. Then read the checklist that you and your teacher will use to evaluate your writing.**

**Directions:** Choose an Olympic athlete who interests you. Write an article about that athlete. Use several sources to gather information, such as books, the Internet, CD-ROMs, newspapers, and magazines. Be sure your explanation is well organized and uses words that make your writing clear.

## Writing Checklist

I will earn my best score if I achieve the following goals:

| | |
|---|---|
| **Ideas** | • Ideas are original<br>• Topic is clearly identified<br>• Ideas support the topic |
| **Organization** | • Ideas are related and presented in correct order<br>• Strong beginning, middle, and end |
| **Creativity and Word Choice** | • Words used appropriately<br>• Creative descriptions<br>• Words enhance ideas |
| **Sentence Structure** | • Complete sentences<br>• Clearly written and easy to understand |
| **Spelling and Punctuation** | • Few or no errors |

# Plan Your Writing

➤ **Use these pages to plan your writing. You may find this graphic organizer helpful.**

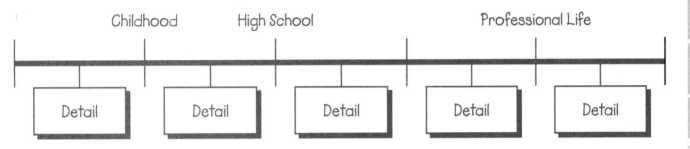

_____

_____

_____

_____

_____

_____

_____

_____

_____

_____

_____

## Writer's Tip

When planning your writing, focus on the main idea. If you are writing a biographical essay, make sure your research emphasizes the main factors in the person's life. For example, if you are writing about a musician, focus on musical training and exposure to music.

_____

_____

_____

# Plan Your Writing

_____

_____

_____

_____

_____

_____

## Writer's Tip

Think carefully about your audience as you gather information. What do they already know? What do you need to explain to them?

_____

_____

_____

_____

_____

_____

_____

_____

_____

_____

## Writer's Tip

Ask a friend to proofread your work for errors. He or she might find mistakes that you missed.

# Write Your Final Draft

> **Use all the skills you have learned in this unit to score well on your final draft. Remember to carefully proofread your work before you give it to your teacher.**

1 _____

2 _____

3 _____

4 _____

5 _____

6 _____

7 _____

8 _____

9 _____

10 _____

11 _____

12 _____

13 _____

14 _____

15 _____

16 _____

17 _____

18 _____

19 _____

20 _____

21 _____

22 _____

23 _____

24 _____

25 _____

26 _____

27 _____

28 _____

29 _____

30 _____

31 _____

32 _____

33 _____

34 _____

35 _____

36 _____

37 _____

38 _____

39 _____

40 _____

41 _____

42 _____

43 _____

44 _____

45 _____

Lesson 6: Your Turn to Write

# Evaluate Your Writing

➤ **Here is the same rubric you used to evaluate Damion's article. Use it to evaluate your writing.**

# Writing Rubric

| Score | Ideas | Organization | Creativity and Word Choice | Sentence Structure | Spelling and Punctuation |
|---|---|---|---|---|---|
| 4 | • Ideas are original<br>• Topic is clearly identified<br>• Ideas support the topic | • Ideas are related and presented in correct order<br>• Strong beginning, middle, and end | • Words used appropriately<br>• Creative descriptions<br>• Words enhance ideas | • Complete sentences<br>• Clearly written and easy to understand | • Few or no errors |
| 3 | • Some ideas are original<br>• Most ideas support the topic | • Most ideas are related and presented in correct order<br>• Good beginning, middle, and end | • Most words used appropriately<br>• Some creative descriptions<br>• Words support ideas | • Many sentences are complete<br>• Most sentences are clearly written and easy to understand | • Some errors |
| 2 | • Few ideas are original<br>• Ideas wander from topic<br>• Some details support the topic | • Some ideas are related and presented in correct order<br>• Weak beginning, middle, and end | • Some words used appropriately<br>• Few creative descriptions | • Some run-on or fragmented sentences<br>• Some sentences are unclear | • Many errors |
| 1 | • Ideas are incomplete<br>• Few details support the topic | • Few ideas are related and presented in correct order<br>• No real beginning, middle, and end | • Few words used appropriately<br>• No attempt at creative descriptions | • Several run-on or fragmented sentences<br>• Many sentences are unclear | • Serious errors |
| 0 | • No attempt | • No attempt | • No attempt | • No attempt | • No attempt |

➤ **Give your own writing a score of 0 to 4 for each category. Explain why you gave yourself that score.**

[ ] score   Ideas _____

_____

_____

[ ] score   Organization _____

_____

_____

[ ] score   Creativity and Word Choice _____

_____

_____

[ ] score   Sentence Structure _____

_____

_____

[ ] score   Spelling and Punctuation _____

_____

_____

# Helpful Tips

| Editing Symbols | | Examples |
|---|---|---|
| ⊙ | Insert a period | We went to the beach⊙<br>I found lots of shells. |
| ⌄ | Insert a comma | Our friend, Tawanda‸is having a party. |
| ∧ | Insert a letter, word, phrase, or sentence | very<br>It is cold outside.<br>∧ |
| ℘ | Take out a letter, word, or phrase | We want ice cream ~~today~~ for dessert. |
| ≡ | Change a lower-case letter to a capital letter | I saw mrs. file yesterday.<br>≡ ≡ |
| / | Change a capital letter to a lower-case letter | We are going to the Movies tonight. |
| ⬭SP | Check the spelling of the word | SP<br>My litle brother is coming with us. |

| Use the correct punctuation mark at the end of every sentence | |
|---|---|
| Use a period for a statement or command: | I brought my lunch today. |
| Use a question mark for a question: | What is in your lunch? |
| Use an exclamation point for a sentence with feeling: | That is my favorite movie! |
| **Use a comma** | |
| between words in a list: | I have a dog, a cat, and a goldfish. |
| between two short sentences: | I was almost late, but I got there. |
| **Use an apostrophe** | |
| in contractions: | didn't (did not);  I'm (I am) |
| in words that show ownership: | dog's tail;  girls' team |